ZAPS: Norton Psychology Labs Workbook

ZAPS: Norton Psychology Labs Workbook

To accompany ZAPS: Norton Psychology Labs at wwnorton.com/zaps

Lauretta Reeves

UNIVERSITY OF TEXAS, AUSTIN

W • W • NORTON & COMPANY • NEW YORK • LONDON

ISBN 13: 978-0-393-93105-6 (pbk.)

W. W. Norton & Company, Inc., 500 Fifth Avenue, New York, N.Y. 10110
www.wwnorton.com
W. W. Norton & Company Ltd., Castle House, 75/76 Wells Street,
London W1T 3QT

9 0

Contents

2-4-6 Task   1

Ames Room   5

Attentional Blink   9

Balance Scale Task   13

Big Five Personality Traits   17

Bipolar Disorder   21

Brown-Peterson Task   25

Classical Conditioning   29

Cognitive Dissonance   33

Concept Formation   39

Conservation   43

Decision Making   47

Dissociative Identity Disorder   51

Emotional Stroop   55

Encoding Specificity   59

False Memory   63

Fan Effect   67

Feature Net   71

Gate Control Theory   75

Genetics   79

Gestalt Problem Solving 85

Iconic Memory 89

Implicit Learning 93

Lateral Inhibition 97

Lexical Decision Task 101

Memory Bias 105

Memory Span 109

Mental Rotation, 2-D 113

Mental Rotation, 3-D 117

Mental Scanning 121

Misconceptions 125

Missionaries and Cannibals 129

Moral Development 135

Obsessive-Compulsive Disorder 139

Operation Span 143

Ponzo Illusion 147

Prisoner's Dilemma 151

Recalling Information 157

Recognizing Emotions 161

Selection Procedure/I.Q. Test 165

Selective Attention 171

Sentence Verification 175

Serial Position Task 179

Signal Detection 183

Signal Detection II 187

Simon Effect 191

Spatial Cueing 195

Split Brain 199

Stereotypes 203

Sternberg Search   207

Stroop Effect   211

Syllogisms   215

Synaptic Transmission   219

Visual Search   223

Wason Selection Task   227

Word Frequency   233

Word Superiority Effect   237

ZAPS | 2-4-6 Task

> **HOW TO:** For each trial, the computer has a rule in mind, and it is your job to guess this rule. Do this by inputting sequences of 3 numbers. The computer will give you feedback as to whether that sequence conforms to the rule. When you think you have figured the rule out, click the **red triangle** to choose among several rules that you think the computer has in mind. You will receive feedback as to whether this rule is correct or not. If not, you will be given more opportunities to input number sequences and thereby induce the correct rule.

You attend a party with your friend James, who remarks, "See that brown-haired woman in the corner? Her name is Gwen, and she's really stuck up." You observe Gwen for a while and see her chat to two people, then snub a man who just arrived at the party. "Aha," you think, "she *is* stuck up!" Why might you conclude that, when you have two pieces of evidence that Gwen is sociable and only one piece of evidence that she snubs people? Why are you willing to confirm your friend James's impression of Gwen? This is an example of **inductive reasoning**—you observe several specific instances of Gwen's behavior, and then induce a general principle from those instances. However, your conclusion about Gwen is based on James's impressions.

Wason's 2-4-6 problem is also an inductive reasoning problem: based on several instances, you are asked to designate a general rule under which those numbers are operating. Just as we induce that tigers are orange with stripes from having seen multiple tigers on TV and from trips to the zoo, you are asked to generate number sequences *to test* whether the rule you have in mind is the same as the one the computer has in mind. Note that true scientific testing dictates that you generate not only sequences that *would* fit the hypothesized rule, but also those that would *not* fit the hypothesized rule (just to make sure you are correct). Here is where many people fail: we are more concerned with confirming our biases and beliefs than with disconfirming them. This is known as the **confirmation bias**.

But, what is the problem with a confirmation bias? In the case of Gwen, thinking that she is stuck up may make you less likely to seek her friendship, when she actually might have proved to be a great friend. Mainly, it prevents you from considering other alternative explanations for her behavior. Perhaps the man she appeared to snub was her abusive ex-boyfriend. Or perhaps she had never been introduced to the man before. Perhaps she smiled at the man as he came in, and you didn't see her friendly behavior.

There are other circumstances in which trying to confirm a hypothesis has even further-reaching consequences. In science, it is very important *not* to fall prey to the confirmation bias. Think about how an experiment is conducted. The experimenter formulates a hypothesis: "People who use visual mnemonics will remember more words from a list than those who use rehearsal." The alternate, **null hypothesis** states: "There will be no difference between the visual mnemonics and the rehearsal groups." Half the subjects are told to use visual mnemonics to remember a list of 20 words; half are told to simply mentally repeat the 20 words over and over again to remember them. The data is collected, and the visual mnemonic group recalls almost twice as many words as the rehearsal group. How does the experimenter report the results? He or she *rejects the null hypothesis*. In other words, the scientist emphasizes that he or she has *dis*confirmed the null hypothesis (rather than confirmed the experimental hypothesis).

Karl Popper, a philosopher of science, emphasized that any good hypothesis should be able to be falsified. This, in fact, has been one of the criticisms of Freud's psychoanalytic theory. Imagine a man comes into a therapist's office and complains that he has low self-esteem and thus is unable to get involved with a woman. The psychoanalytic therapist says, "This is because you have not worked through your Oedipus complex. You are still worried that you are attracted to your mother, and that your father is a rival for your mother's affections. This unconscious conflict is causing your low self-esteem and shyness around women." The man thanks the therapist, leaves, and comes back to his therapy session the next week angry. "I don't have sexual feelings for my mother, nor do I think of my father as a rival. My low self-esteem is due to having been bullied in school as a child." The therapist looks at the angry man and says, "See—your anger shows that you are defensive about having unconscious sexual feelings for your mother." The therapist thus exhibits the confirmation bias. By not considering alternative explanations for the man's low self-esteem, he is unable to help the man.

ZAPS: 2-4-6 TASK

Questions

1. Do you think that there is an evolutionary reason (or explanation) for why people would exhibit a confirmation bias but not seek disconfirming evidence for their views?

2. How do you think that the confirmation bias might affect jury decision making in trials? Is it more likely to help or to hinder justice?

3. What area of education might help people overcome their tendencies to engage in the confirmation bias? Mathematics? Logic? Science? Or specific training about biases in decision making?

ZAPS | # Ames Room

How to: Press the **Start** button to view a room through a peephole. Press the **Girl** and **Boy** buttons to make them change places. Try this several times. Then press the **Continue** button to see the view 3-dimensionally. By pressing **Floor**, **Ceiling**, **Wall**, you will be able to see how the room is constructed to mislead you.

Have you ever been in a carnival funhouse, with trick mirrors that make objects close by look far away and far-away things look close by? Or mirrors that make your middle look abnormally thin or thick? Has a car parked next to you ever started to back out, and you assume that instead your car is rolling forward? Sometimes things are not what they seem. Now imagine that you are friends with identical twins, Tweedledum and Tweedledee, both of whom are approaching you from down the street. One is a block away, the other is half a block away. How can you tell which one is closer? What cues do you automatically use without consciously realizing it?

The closer twin, Tweedledum, looms larger in our retinal image than the farther-away Tweedledee. When 2 individuals we know to be the same size appear to be different sizes, the mind automatically uses this information to calculate that one is farther away.

Most of the time, this calculation will provide an accurate portrayal of the world. But not in the **Ames Room**, which was invented by opthamologist Adelbert Ames to illustrate a visual illusion. There are actually 2 illusions in the Ames Room. The first has to do with the apparent shape of the room itself. When looking through a peephole into the Ames Room, our limited view allows us to interpret the room as the same evenly proportioned square as most other rooms. However, as you will see in the ZAP demonstration, 2 of the walls are actually trapezoid-shaped, making the left back corner farther away than the right back corner. Thus the walls are not perfectly perpendicular to the floor. The floor also slopes downward toward the left corner. Because only one eye can look through the peephole, the abnormal structure of the room is not obvious—the floor appears level, and the room looks like a standard cube. Our prior knowledge also comes into play—we are used to seeing square rooms and so expect to see a standard cubic room, making our visual system biased toward a square-room interpretation.

Normally, we are subject to a perceptual constancy known as **size constancy**: We conclude that people and objects remain the same size even when they are nearer and farther from us. Thus, even though Tweedledee appears smaller to us in the earlier example, we know he hasn't really changed size. Because of size constancy, we know objects and people don't shrink or grow larger sporadically; we interpret the "smaller" Tweedledee as being farther away than the "larger" Tweedledum.

However, in the Ames Room illusion, distance cues and size constancy compete with each other, and distance cues win. With this second visual illusion, our mind performs an opposite calculation than what is usual. Normally, we use relative size to compute the distance of people or objects from us. However, the Ames Room tricks us into interpreting the 2 back corners of the room as equidistant from us (which they are not). Thus, when 2 people appear to be standing equal distances away from us in the Ames Room, we assume that the person in the farther corner must be smaller (because he or she produces a smaller retinal image). Because viewing the trapezoidal room through a peephole obscures normal distance and perspective information, as a person moves from the closer corner to the farther corner and back, he seems to shrink and then grow larger. Illusory visual cues override size constancy in the Ames Room.

ZAPS: AMES ROOM

Questions

1. Look at an object (or person) close to you, and a similar one farther away. What differences are there in your perceptions of the 2 stimuli? Does it require both eyes to ascertain the relative distance of the 2 objects from you?

2. What relationship does the Ames Room have to other visual illusions, such as the Muller-Lyer and the Ponzo Illusions? How do the explanations for each illusion overlap with or differ from each other?

ZAPS | Attentional Blink

> **How to:** On each trial, a fixation point will appear in the middle of the screen. Sixteen numbers, interspersed with a few letters, will appear in very fast succession. Your job is to remember the letters and to type them in at the end of the trial. Be as accurate as possible; speed is not measured in this experiment. There are 3 practice trials, followed by 80 test trials.

You are seated in class, happily taking notes on organic chemistry, when a loud noise interrupts your concentration. Everyone in the class diverts their attention out the window. However, the professor keeps lecturing. Once you realize that the loud noise was only a car backfiring, and return to note-taking, you realize that you've missed a critical sentence in the professor's lecture.

The moment that you missed is due to a phenomenon known as **attentional blink**. First, your attention is directed to the organic chemistry lecture, then to the loud noise (and not on lecture), then back to lecture. While you are able to take notes on lecture 30 seconds after the loud noise occurs, information that immediately follows the startling noise is lost.

It's well known that many of our cognitive abilities have a **limited capacity**. Nowhere is this more evident than with attention. Most of us would find it difficult to follow 3 conversations at the same time at a party, or to study for an exam effectively while watching TV. Processing information uses both time and mental capacity. While your attention is focused on one thing (a loud noise, a conversation), attention cannot be focused on something else (organic chemistry lecture). The attentional blink illustrates **selective attention**—we often tend to focus on one stimulus and block out other stimuli. Sometimes we may choose to pay attention to one piece of information over another. At other times, the stimulus upon which we focus is determined for us; dramatic events like the loud noise during organic chemistry lecture automatically divert our attention momentarily.

There are, however, situations in which we can demonstrate **divided attention** between two (and sometimes more) stimuli. You can carry on a conversation while driving, or perhaps listen to music while studying. However, divided attention tasks typically lead to greater errors: you may not process information as well if you study while listening to music, and your risk of having an accident while talking on a cell phone is 3 to 5 times greater than if you are not talking on a cell phone while driving (even if you use a headset rather than a hand-held phone). The reason? We are best at processing information one piece at a time, which is what the attentional blink requires us to do.

ZAPS: ATTENTIONAL BLINK

Questions

1. List 3 real-life examples of selective attention, and 3 instances in which your attention was divided.

2. What advantages would there be to having an unlimited attentional capacity? What might be some disadvantages?

3. How is attention connected to memory?

ZAPS | Balance Scale Task

How to: The Experience section of this ZAP counts as your practice. You will see a picture of a balance scale with two containers on either side of the center. Weights will appear below the scale. Put the weights into the containers on the scale, and then press the **See** button to see what happens. You do not need to use all of the weights on each trial, and more than one weight can be placed in each container on the scale. Press **Next** to start a new trial.

When you are ready to begin the official experiment, press **Further**. During each trial of the experiment, a scale with weights will appear. Your task is to judge which side of the scale will go down (because it is heavier), or whether the scale will remain balanced. A happy face or sad face will appear after you have made your judgment to tell you if you are correct or not. Press the **spacebar** to continue to the next trial. There are 20 trials overall.

Hint: In this ZAP, you may recruit younger children (ages 5 years and up) to participate to observe the developmental use of rules in this problem-solving task.

Inhelder and Piaget (1958) posed a **pendulum problem** to children: the children's job was to figure out what factors influence how fast a pendulum will swing. A rod was presented on which strings of various lengths could be hung. The children could then attach objects of different weights to the strings. They were also told that they could vary the force with which they pushed the pendulum and the height from which they dropped the pendulum. Thus there were 4 factors to consider—string length, weight of object, force of pushing, and the height of the dropped pendulum—when trying to determine which variable/s influenced pendulum speed.

Under age 7, very few children arrive at the right answer. Furthermore, they tend to be unsystematic in their testing—they will compare a trial with a long string and light weight to a trial using a short string and heavy weight. This does not enable them to isolate the factor/s relevant to the pendulum problem.

Between ages 7 and 11, children use somewhat more systematic strategies: they will compare 2 different weights using the same length string. However, they announce their conclusions before testing *all* variables and sets of variables. It isn't until age 11 and older that children behave more like scientists by formulating a hypothesis ("Length of string matters, but weight does not") and then test that hypothesis *systematically*. Children this age are included in Piaget's **Formal Operations stage**, and should exhaust all possible factors by comparing string lengths, weights, heights from which the weights are dropped, and so on, before announcing their conclusion.

Piaget's pendulum problem was designed to exhibit developmental differences in children's thinking and use of problem-solving strategies. Likewise, Siegler (1976, 1981) developed the balance scale problem to reveal differences in children's use of rules in problem solving. Initially, Siegler thought that children would exhibit stage-like progression, first using simple rules in the Balance Scale Task and progressing to the use of increasingly sophisticated rules. However, he now advocates an **adaptive strategy-choice model**, which states that children at a given age may have *several* strategies they consider, and these strategies compete for use. Thus, even older children may consider simple rules (and occasionally use them), but will be better able to use complex rules when the task requires them. Siegler can thus account for why children become better and more systematic at problem-solving tasks: they consider more complex rules and use them as necessary. His model also accounts for the gradual improvement in problem-solving strategies; cognitive abilities tend not to improve as abruptly as Piaget's "stages" implies.

ZAPS: BALANCE SCALE TASK

Questions

1. Think about how a younger brother or sister (or niece or nephew) plays strategy games like Monopoly, Battleship, chess, or checkers. Can you discern any rules that the younger person is using? How have your strategies in these games changed as you have grown older or practiced the games more?

2. How much of the improvement of problem-solving strategies is due to development versus greater experience and expertise in a task (such as playing chess)? Can a child show adept problem-solving strategies in one activity while showing substandard performance on other types of problems?

ZAPS | Big Five Personality Traits

> **How to:** You will be presented with 100 sentences that you must judge on a 1 to 5 scale, with 1 = the statement does not apply to me at all, up to 5 = the statement applies to me entirely (or any gradient response in between).

Personality forms a major basis for how we think of ourselves, how we classify other people, and how we predict how we or others might behave in a given situation. For example, our friend Jillian may be considered friendly and sociable, funny and intelligent. We might then predict that she would be a good person to invite to a dinner party because she will respond positively to the other guests and liven up the party. Alternately, we might consider ourselves shy and introverted and realize that it is best to invite only a few people to our dinner party and to make sure that we invite some sociable people (like Jillian) to ensure conversation.

Notice that when we think of ourselves ("introverted") or others ("sociable," "funny"), we do so with personality *traits* that imply a certain consistency of behavior across time and situations. Thus, we label Jillian "sociable" because for the 2 years we've known her, she usually has an easy time chatting to people (consistent across time). Furthermore, we've seen her be chatty at parties, during study groups, in the dorm, and when talking to professors (consistent across situations).

Most research on personality is based on the measurement of traits, and most people agree that some traits are more central than others. The "Big Five" personality traits are those that psychologists consider basic and that help predict lower-level traits and behaviors. For example, if we know that Samuel is high on "Openness to Experience" (one of the Big Five traits), then he might be more willing to try skydiving than stodgy Frederick.

The Big Five personality traits targeted by McCrae and Costa (1987, 1997, 1999), and their sub-traits, are:

1. *Extraversion:* Extraverts are sociable, fun-loving, assertive people who prefer a high activity level and exhibit largely positive emotions.
2. *Neuroticism* (the opposite of Emotional Stability measured in the ZAP): People who are high in Neuroticism are often anxious, worried, or depressed, tend to be very self-conscious and insecure, and may exhibit impulsiveness and hostility on occasion.
3. *Conscientiousness:* Conscientious people have a strong sense of duty and a need to achieve. They exhibit self-discipline and a desire for order and predictability.
4. *Agreeableness:* Those deemed agreeable are honest and compliant. They try to make social relations smooth, and exhibit altruism and tenderness toward others.
5. *Openness to Experience:* Those who are high on Openness have unconventional values, are independent and imaginative, and prefer a variety of experiences. They tend to have artistic interests and an active imagination.

There is evidence that these Big Five traits are good at describing the personalities of people from different countries and cultures, and even at describing the personalities of some animals (Gosling & John, 1999).

Personality tests, such as the one in the ZAP, have usually been *standardized,* so that a pattern of responding to some questions correlates highly with a personality trait. For example, if there are 20 questions on a personality test relevant to Extraversion, then people who respond to most of those questions will be deemed "Extraverted." How do the authors of the test know for certain that these 20 questions related to Extraversion? They may have tested a number of people that others deemed "Extraverted" and a number that others deemed "Introverted." If the Extraverts tended to answer "yes" to the 20 questions, and the Introverts tended to answer "no," then those 20 questions may be a valid way to categorize people on the Extraversion trait. (Notice, however, that someone may not need to answer all 20 questions "yes" to be an Extravert—the *pattern* of responses is measured.)

ZAPS: BIG FIVE PERSONALITY TRAITS

Questions

1. Did you score as you expected on each of the Big Five traits? Would those who know you best—friends and family—agree with the assessment of the Big Five personality test?

2. Think of pets you've had—do they exhibit behaviors that could be classified as any of the Big Five personality traits? Are these the same behaviors that people would have to exhibit to be labeled Extraverted, or Agreeable?

3. Do you think that 5 major personality traits are enough to encapsulate all of a person's personality? What factors may have been left out of the Big Five theory of personality?

ZAPS | # Bipolar Disorder

> **How to:** The 10 assignments in this ZAP are interspersed with a sequence of video clips of a man with a mood disorder. During each assignment, answer the questions as best you can and click the **Check** button to test your answers. You may replay the videos as necessary by pressing the **Video** button.

Both bipolar disorder and major (or unipolar) depression are considered mood disorders under the *DSM-IV*. Depression is sometimes referred to as the "common cold" of mental illness because of its prevalence. It is estimated that at least 20% of women and 10% of men will suffer from unipolar depression at some point in their lives. Some forms of major depression clearly have a genetic basis and run in families. Most cases, however, cannot be traced to a genetic cause, but are induced by neurotransmitter or hormone fluctuations (such as postpartum depression, brought on by hormonal irregularities after childbirth) or environmental causes (a romantic break-up, death of a loved one, or chronic stress). Seligman (1974) proposed that many incidents of depression are caused by "learned helplessness," in which a person feels that she cannot do anything to help herself out of a bad situation and thus gives up.

Bipolar depression (formerly known as manic depression), on the other hand, affects only 1% of the population, and there is strong evidence for a genetic basis of this disorder. Sufferers alternate between periods of depression and anxiety and manic phases in which they have a lot of energy. While the manic stage sounds as if it might be useful (especially during finals week), it has significant drawbacks. People during the manic stage may feel euphoric, but just as often are irritable, unable to focus, and exhibit poor judgment. Their family, co-workers, and friends may find them difficult to be around.

A link between bipolar depression and creativity has been proposed because many famous artists, such as Georgia O'Keeffe and Vincent Van Gogh; authors, such as Edgar Allan Poe; poets, such as Lord Byron; and composers, such as Robert Schumann, suffered from manic depression. However, while manic phases do make people engage in flights of fancy that might propel creativity, research has found that most of the best work of artists may actually take place during *hypomania* periods (*hypo* = beneath), when their mood and energy levels are only slightly elevated. During full manic periods, people do not necessarily have the attention span or self-discipline to be productive, or to evaluate the quality of the work that they are producing.

Name: _____

Class: _____

Professor: _____

Date: _____

ZAPS: BIPOLAR DISORDER

Questions

1. Why does the evidence suggest that manic depression (or bipolar disorder) has more of a genetic basis than unipolar (or major) depression?

2. What aspects of how one is raised might increase the likelihood that a propensity toward manic depression will become a full-blown mental illness? What factors during adulthood might exacerbate manic or depressive episodes?

3. What psychological/lifestyle and physiological factors might explain why women are more likely to suffer from major (or unipolar) depression?

HOW TO: On each trial, you will see three characters (called a **triad**) presented briefly. Then a single letter will be presented—press the **c**-key if that letter is a consonant, the **m**-key if it is a vowel. Individual letters will keep appearing for between 2 and 20 seconds—make a consonant (c-key)/vowel (m-key) decision about each one as it appears. Finally, a matrix of letters will appear per trial. Click on the letters you saw in the triad in the order that you saw them (from left to right). Click **Continue** to go to the next trial. Your data will appear at the end.

Imagine you meet your friend Jason on the way back to the dorm after a run. He says, "I just moved—my new phone number is 482-6127." Since you are in jogging clothes with no pen with which to write down Jason's new phone number, you try to keep it active in short-term memory while you run up the stairs to your dorm room. How likely are you to remember his phone number if you live on the second floor? On the third floor? On the fourth floor of the dorm? After all, it will take you longer to get to a pen the higher up you live. What will happen to your memory if another friend stops to ask if you want to go to dinner later? The question posed in this demonstration is how long does information in short-term memory last before it is lost or forgotten?

One assumption in asking this question is that information in STM fades, or decays with time. Brown (1958) and Peterson & Peterson (1959) both used a task designed to test the duration of short-term memory. They gave people a trigram (string of 3 letters) to remember. However, to prevent rehearsal, they asked people to count backwards by 3s from a given number. If given "CVL" to remember, followed by "99," subjects were told to count "99, 96, 93, 90, 87, 84 . . ." until signaled to stop and immediately recall the trigram. What Brown and the Petersons manipulated was the length of time between when subjects heard the trigram, and when they were asked to recall it. Intervals were 0 seconds between trigram and recall, 3 seconds, 6, 9, 12, 15, or 18 seconds. What the researchers found was a consistent downward curve—less information was remembered the longer the time interval. By 18 seconds, subjects had lost nearly all information about the trigram.

So short-term memory lasts less than 20 seconds, right? Reitman (1971; 1974), however, argued that *interference*, not *decay*, was responsible for subjects' forgetting of the trigram by 18 seconds. Counting backwards by 3s displaces, or interferes with, memory for the trigram. The interference is especially great because the trigram is a verbal stimulus, and counting backward by 3s is a verbal task. Two pieces of verbal information are more likely to interfere with each other than a verbal and a nonverbal task.

What if subjects didn't do anything during the 0, 3, 6, 9, 12, 15, or 18-second interval (but were told not to rehearse)? What if they had to perform a nonverbal interference task? Reitman gave subjects 3 4-letter words ("tree") to remember on each trial. Half the subjects listened to white noise for 15 seconds; the other half heard a 15-second tape recording of repeated "toh toh toh . . ." in which an occasional "doh" was heard, and they were to press a button when they heard each "doh." After 15 seconds, the recall rate was 92% for those in the tone group, but only 77% for those in the syllable group. Having to listen to white noise did not cause loss of the 3 words, but performing a verbal task (toh/doh task) did.

Thus, while some still believe that decay causes loss of information in STM—information that we do not rehearse or to which we do not pay attention, can be lost—most researchers now think that interference is the main reason information is lost in STM. In other words, you're more likely to forget your friend's new phone number while running upstairs to your dorm room if someone talks to you than if you have to run up 4 flights of stairs.

Name: _____

Class: _____

Professor: _____

Date: _____

ZAPS: BROWN-PETERSON TASK

Questions

1. Based on your own experience, do you think that loss of information from short-term memory is due more to decay or to interference? What about loss of information in long-term memory?

2. How difficult is it not to rehearse when you know that you are being tested for your memory? Is it possible to keep your mind entirely blank for up to 20 or 30 seconds? How might a person's ability to do so impact the results of the Brown-Peterson experiment?

3. Would the tasks that Brown-Peterson and Reitman used have any impact on people's short-term memory for a set of numbers, or a sequence of visual colors? Explain.

ZAPS | Classical Conditioning

> **How to:** This ZAP allows you to recreate a classical conditioning experiment in the context of stimuli that make a dog salivate. Click on one or several objects (lamp, bell, meat) to use in your first experiment. Click **Start** and the results of the experiment appear in the left-hand window. Each time you press Start, the dog receives a new exposure to the stimulus/stimuli you have chosen. Present the stimuli multiple times to the dog by pressing Start; the cumulative effects of the experiment appear in the right-hand window.
>
> If you want to begin a new experiment with a fresh dog, press the **Restart** button again, and select a new set of objects.

You and your sister Stephanie pay for your tickets to see *Friday the Thirteenth, Part 34* and, with trepidation, find your seats in the dark theater. The movie begins showing some teenagers camping out in the woods. As they sit around a campfire, you start to hear ominous music, da dum . . . da dum . . . . You grab Stephanie's arm and notice that your heart is pounding out of your chest. Why? Instead of waiting for Serial Killer Jason to appear, your stress response occurs *before* any murder takes place in the movie.

Let's think about how this might have happened. It is estimated that an average 13-year-old has viewed 8,000 murders and 100,000 acts of violence on TV or in movies. Chances are that many (if not most) of those TV murders have been preceded by ominous music. It is a natural response to show physiological anxiety (faster heart rate, increased blood pressure, a desire to flee) when confronted with violence. Over time, though, we learn to **associate** violence and the ominous music. As a result, the ominous music alone leads to a stress reaction.

Russian psychologist Ivan Pavlov was the first to discover and explore the principles of learning associations within **classical conditioning**. While studying dog's salivation after being presented with food or meat powder, he noticed that the dogs would salivate when the research assistants entered the room (but before the dogs had been given any food). At first, Pavlov was irritated because this was ruining his carefully controlled experiments. However, he then realized that this early salivation by the dogs was interesting in its own right. It is natural for a dog to salivate (an unlearned, or **unconditioned response (UCR)**) to meat powder (the **unconditioned stimulus (UCS)**). Once the dogs associated the research assistants with the provision of meat powder, the research assistant became a learned, or **conditioned stimulus (CS)**. Salivation to the research assistant was the **conditioned response (CR)**. Pavlov then set out to explore this new type of automated learning.

Likewise, your pounding heart in *Friday the Thirteenth, Part 34* is due to classical conditioning. A fear response to seeing violence is natural—fear and a pounding heart are the UCRs; seeing violence is the UCS. Once you learn the connection between the ominous music and violence, the music serves as a CS for a fear response (the CR). Notice that the UCR and CR are the same behaviors, but are elicited by different stimuli—the UCS or CS, respectively.

ZAPS: CLASSICAL CONDITIONING

Questions

1. When does your anxiety over an exam start in earnest? After you read an exam question for which you don't know the answer, or before that (perhaps as the test is being handed out). Explain your test anxiety in terms of classical conditioning.

2. Classical conditioning has been found even in very simple animals. Why might it be adaptive in terms of survival?

3. Take notes on some of the advertising to which you are exposed over the course of a week. What are some examples of classical conditioning that advertisers use, to get you to associate their product/s with pleasant things or events? Explain each example, using classical conditioning terminology.

ZAPS | Cognitive Dissonance

HOW TO: There are three phases to this ZAP. In the first, you will see a list of sentences stating either positive (+) or negative (−) relationships between the three objects/people in the triangle (labeled O, P, and X). At the bottom of the page are triangles depicting various positive/negative relationships among three points of a triangle. Drag the letter of each sentence to the triangle best exemplifying the positive/negative relationships in the sentence. You will receive feedback when finished.

In the second assignment, you will have to say whether the triads are in balance or not. Drag the Imbalanced triads at the bottom of the page to the left side of the page and the Balanced triads to the right side of the page.

The third assignment asks you to change the Imbalanced triads into Balanced triads by reading the sentence in red beneath each statement and then clicking on which + or − sign in that triad should be changed (in accordance with the sentence in red).

Leon Festinger was puzzled by widespread rumors in a village in India that there was going to be another earthquake, shortly after an earthquake had devastated that same village. Why would the people deliberately make themselves anxious, when there was no scientific evidence that another earthquake was imminent? Festinger hypothesized that the rumors were actually a way for people to *justify* their persistent anxiety—the rumors allowed them to have a reason for continuing to feel tense. The theory of Cognitive Dissonance was born.

Dissonance theory makes several claims:

1. We prefer our beliefs, attitudes, and behaviors to be consistent. If we strongly believe in the right to vote, then we don't miss an election. This part of the theory was based on Heider's Balance theory, which claims that any set of relationships among three objects and/or people is characterized by positive or negative relationships. Relationships are balanced if the overall valence is positive (as in + + +, or + − − triads) or imbalanced if the overall valences is negative (− − −, or + + −). Heider's theory formed the basis for this ZAP experience.

2. When we become aware of inconsistencies, we are motivated to make our cognitions, attitudes, and behaviors consistent. We can do this either by finding some external justification (we missed voting because we had flu; the people in the Indian village manufactured an earthquake rumor to justify their anxiety) or by changing one of the cognitions, behaviors, or attitudes. For instance, if we miss voting in an election, we could alter our attitudes about the importance of voting.

Sometimes cognitive dissonance theory leads to surprising results. Festinger and Carlsmith (1959) asked undergraduates to perform a boring task (turning knobs clockwise and counterclockwise) for 1 hour. Afterward, the experimenter asked each subject to tell the person scheduled next, out in the waiting room, that the experiment was actually interesting. Half the subjects were paid $1 for this favor, and the other half were offered $20 (quite a bit of money to a 1950s college student!). All agreed. When interviewed later, the $1 subjects actually reported more satisfaction from the boring experiment than did the $20 subjects. How could this be? According to cognitive dissonance theory, if asked why they had agreed to lie to the person in the waiting room (given that most of us think of ourselves as honest), the $20 subjects could say, "Because I was promised a lot of money to do so!" They thus had sufficient justification for the discrepancy between their self-image as honest and their lying behavior. The $1 subjects, though, had no such rationale. The dissonance induced by lying, even though they probably considered themselves honest, could be resolved by *not* really having lied—the task actually *was* interesting! In this case, behavior actually changed an attitude—saying that a task was interesting led to believing that the task was interesting, *as long as there was not sufficient external justification ($20) for the behavior.*

In another experiment, Rokeach (1971) asked students to rank order a list of 18 values, including *Freedom* (defined as "independent choice") and *Justice* (defined as "brotherhood"). Half of the subjects who ranked Freedom as more important than Justice were told that they were selfish and more interested in their own liberty than in equal opportunity for all people. This manipulation was designed to induce cognitive dissonance by pointing out that their behavior in the value-ranking task was discrepant from most subjects' self-images as fair. Rokeach then arranged for the NAACP (National Association for the Advancement of Colored People) to send requests for membership to all subjects. Those in the dissonance group, who were told they were selfish for ranking Freedom higher than Justice, were 3 times as likely to join the NAACP as those in the nondissonance group and showed attitude changes up to one-and-a-half years later.

Festinger proposed that cognitive dissonance causes enough discomfort that we are motivated to rectify a dissonant situation or collection of attitudes. Steele (1988), however, has claimed that the main motivation to resolve dissonance is to maintain a positive self-image and sense of self-worth. The $1 subjects in the Festinger and Carlsmith experiment faced having to admit that they were dishonest unless they convinced themselves that the boring experiment was actually interesting. Likewise, subjects in the Rokeach experiment had to admit that they were selfish or racist (or both); joining the NAACP was a way of dispelling concerns about their self-image.

ZAPS: COGNITIVE DISSONANCE

Questions

1. Can you think of a time when you had to re-evaluate an attitude or belief because of dissonance? Try to chart your dissonant attitudes in a Heider-like triad.

2. What will likely happen if a person remains blissfully unaware of a set of dissonant attitudes?

3. Cognitive dissonance theory predicts that you will report the most satisfaction for a job that does *not* pay well. Why? What would a behaviorist predict your job satisfaction would be for a poorly paid position? Is there a way to resolve the 2 views?

| **ZAPS** | Concept Formation |

How to: You will see a card at the left-hand side of the screen, along with 81 other cards. These cards will very in several dimensions—color, number, and border. The card at the top is a member of the mystery category; your task is to figure out which features determine membership in that category. Select one card at a time from the 81 and you will be told if it is an exemplar of the concept (category) or a non-exemplar. Choose carefully, and try to figure out the concept by checking as few cards as possible. Once you think you have figured out which features are important, press the **Concept** button. You will be informed whether you are correct or not. If not, continue with the task until you are able to accurately induce the category rule.

It's Friday night. You and your friends arrive at the hot nightclub that's just opened up in town. The requirements for entry are very strict, but the club refuses to publicize exactly what those requirements are. Rather than risk rejection, you and your friends decide to watch people entering from a distance in order to figure out the entry requirements.

First, a man in a tie is allowed to enter, followed by a man without a tie. Next, a woman in pants is denied entry, but a woman in a skirt is permitted entry. Then, a man wearing only a shirt and pants is allowed to enter. After an hour of observation, you and your friends conclude that the rule is that women must be wearing a skirt, but that any man may enter.

Bruner and his colleagues (1956) began testing people's ability to induce general category rules from feedback on which exemplars are *in* the category and which exemplars are *out*. There are four basic rules that are tested in such concept formation tasks. The easiest is the **conjunctive rule**: an exemplar must have traits *A and B* to be considered in a category (e.g., must have passed Introduction to Psychology and Statistics to take a psychology lab course). Another rule is the **disjunctive rule**, which says that *either A or B* must apply (you must have passed Introduction to Psychology or tested out of it to take an upper-level course).

Somewhat more difficult are *conditional* rules, such as the ones for entry into the posh new club. A conditional rule can be phrased in "If . . ., then . . ." terms (such as "If you are a woman, then you must be wearing a skirt"). Conditional rules are harder to learn because they also entail that those exemplars (or people) to whom the rule does not apply *all* belong to the category. Thus, women must be wearing a skirt to enter the nightclub, but the rule says nothing about men. Thus, all men are allowed to enter (regardless of their dress). *Biconditional* rules include both a conditional injunction *and* its inverse, "If you are a woman, then you must be wearing a skirt, *and* if you are wearing a skirt, then you must be a woman." Men in skirts would be admitted under the conditional nightclub rule, but *not* under the biconditional rule. Within the ZAP, you can also learn about different strategies for figuring out the rules in concept formation tasks.

The benefit of concept formation tasks using well-defined criteria is that experimenters can manipulate the stimuli systematically, and figure out which types of concept rules are easiest for people to master. However, one criticism of such experiments is that, in real life, there are rarely concepts with strict laws as to which items belong to a category, and which items don't. Think of fruits: many fruits are roundish in shape (but bananas are not); most have seeds inside that are evident (but coconuts themselves are the seeds, and strawberries' seeds are on the outside). Furthermore, while most fruits have a high sugar content, tomatoes, cucumbers, and olives (all technically fruit) will probably never appear in a fruit salad or as yogurt flavors.

ZAPS: CONCEPT FORMATION

Questions

1. Which of the strategies detailed in the ZAP did you adopt? Explain.

2. Formulate a conjunctive, disjunctive, conditional, and biconditional rule for the types of apartments in which you're willing to live.

ZAPS | Conservation

Remember having spinach for dinner as a child? Your parents may have forced you to eat everything on your plate, especially your vegetables. After a few awful mouthfuls, you spread the remaining spinach around on your plate and said to your parents, "See how much I ate? Am I done?"

Why would spreading the remaining spinach around on your plate fool your parents into letting you off the hook? Why would you believe that it would work?

Piaget was interested in how people, especially children, reasoned about the physical world. One of his classic tasks was a conservation task, in which he presented children with two quantities of liquid (or clay or objects)—say, one tall glass of *red* water and an identical glass of *blue* water. One of the quantities—the *blue*—was altered in look, such as having one of the liquids poured into a shallow, wide container. Piaget found that children under age 7 would claim that the quantity had changed, that now there was more *red* water because it was taller. These pre-conservation children were said to engage in **centration**—the tendency to focus on one element of the problem (e.g., what the two quantities look like). Thus, they ignore that nothing is added or taken away during the liquid transformation, and concentrate on the fact that one of the liquids looks taller than the other. (Piaget's task works even if children claim that the *blue* liquid now has more because "It looks wider.")

Depending on the conservation task, Piaget found that children over age seven typically passed conservation tasks, because they realized that a perceptual transformation did not change the *quantity* of liquid (or clay or the number of objects). Making something shorter or wider or taller does not change *how much* of a substance there is. However, children do not come to an understanding of conservation all at one time. They may attain liquid and mass conservation at age 7, but conservation of area not until age 8 or 9. Piaget termed this incremental, step-like attainment of a skill **horizontal decalage**.

So what would make your parents think you'd eaten more of your spinach than you actually had? After all, Piaget found that children over age 7 should pass conservation tasks. We can all agree that food spread out on a plate *looks* like less than the same food in a single pile. Thus, if your parents didn't see you spread out your spinach, they were not privy to the transformation in the same way that Piaget's child subjects were. This may have allowed them to believe that you had eaten more spinach than you actually had (or perhaps they simply took pity on you!).

Name: _____

Class: _____

Professor: _____

Date: _____

ZAPS: CONSERVATION

Questions

1. Can you think of ways in which young children illustrate their lack of conservation skills (e.g., getting upset if offered a short glass of milk)?

2. What other types of logical thinking accompany 7- to 8-year-olds who are beginning to pass conservation? What types of mathematical skills might result from a greater understanding of conservation?

3. How could you promote conservation skills in children? How much training would it take to get a 5-year-old to pass conservation tasks, in your estimation (if possible at all)?

ZAPS | Decision Making

> **HOW TO:** You will be asked to solve a number of reasoning problems (some of which may sound very similar to each other). Read each problem and answer it carefully. You will be given feedback on your responses at the end of the ZAP.

When was the last time you had to make a monumental decision? Which used car to buy with your graduation money? Whether to attend your high school prom or the regional track meet? Whether to relax during semester break or get a part-time job? Some ̃es, we consider all of our alternatives objectively before making a decisio. Other times, we are influenced by emotional factors (such when the de̤ to sleep in for seven days straight wins out over the extra money from a j̤ ̃uring semester break). While making some decisions, statistical data m̤ ̃eavily influences our final decision. For example, we may compare the ̤ ̃bility records of two cars we want to buy, or find out the statistical odds of ̤ ̃plications from the flu itself versus complications from getting a flu shot. C̤ ̃ decisions are made based on a single piece of information from a frien̤ ̃hat car looks outdated"), or anecdotal evidence (a friend who says, "I go̤ ̃u shot last year, but still got sick with the flu!").

Research on decision making has shown that people engag̤ systematic reasoning biases. We tend to reason in non-mathematical ways̤ to alter our decisions based on how a problem is stated. For example, a den̤ ̃night be more likely to convince you to undergo a root canal if she says t̤ ̃he has a 95% success rate, with no complications, versus telling you that ̤ ̃ is a 5% chance of complications. Even though the two statements convey ̤ same success to risk ratio, somehow the "95% success rate" sounds more comforting. More people buy lottery tickets when a state lottery jackpot reaches the $250 million range (even though the chances of winning have now decreased because so many more tickets have been sold).

One might expect that people would always try to maximize their gains in any decision-making scenario. However, this predicts that they should pay attention to statistical probabilities when calculating gains versus risk (and the evidence suggests people do not always pay attention to statistical probabilities). It also leaves open the possibility that the person will suffer the same fate as the dog with a bone in Aesop's fable: A dog carrying a bone in its mouth came upon a river. As it saw its own reflection in the water, it grew envious that the reflected dog had a bone, too. As the dog unwittingly snapped at his own reflection in order to gain two bones, it dropped its real bone and ended up with nothing.

Alternately, we might expect people to merely minimize their losses, and always take the safe course. This would mean that they seek to hold on to what they have at the expense of gaining even bigger rewards. People who hide their money under the mattress, rather than putting it into a savings account on which it can draw interest, fall into this camp.

As you will see in this ZAP, people are not always purely logical decision makers, and do show a tendency to make reasoning "errors" in that their decisions are different from what a mathematician or economist would suggest is the best course of action. There are also vast individual differences in how people reason. Some people like the thrill of a gamble, while others prefer safe choices.

ZAPS: DECISION MAKING

Questions

1. Why is it hard for people to reason statistically? Do you think that more advanced training in math, economics, and statistics would lead people to think more economically in real life?

2. Can you pick out occasions in which you exhibited any of the reasoning biases or heuristics covered in this ZAP?

3. We often warn ourselves (and others) about making decisions based on our emotional reactions. Why do you think emotions might cloud our judgment and prevent us from being rational? Or, is it possible that emotions serve a useful purpose during decision making? Can you think of any examples where your emotions were more accurate than your intellect during a decision?

ZAPS | Dissociative Identity Disorder

How to: The 8 assignments in this ZAP are alternated with video clips of people with dissociative identity disorder. Press the **space bar** to begin each section, and answer the questions posed to you in the assignments. Press the **Check** button to get feedback about your answers.

In movies, murder suspects sometimes fake having multiple personalities to get acquitted or to be judged "not guilty by reason of insanity." Is it possible? Could someone merely pretend to have 2, or 3, or more personalities, with the main personality not knowing what the other ones were up to?

Imagine you were the prosecutor who wanted to make sure that the suspect went to jail for a long time for perpetrating a hideous crime. Are there techniques that you could use (or that the court psychologist could use) to determine that the suspect is faking? What aspects of a person's childhood might the psychologist be interested in finding out?

Dissociative identity disorder (DID) is a rare but serious mental illness where a person dissociates significantly enough from his/her personality to be considered to have multiple "personalities" inhabiting the same body. Sometimes the dominant personality is aware of the others, but often is not. The personalities may have different names, and even exhibit different physiological responses (such as blood pressure, or even eye color!). Some of the alter-identities may be diametrically opposed to the dominant personality in terms of extroversion/introversion, levels of aggression, sexual orientation. The other personalities may be of a different gender, race, or age.

Some therapists remain skeptical about the truth of dissociative identity disorder, claiming that psychologists and psychiatrists may help the patient "construct" multiple personalities, and then continue to reinforce the person with extra attention being paid to their dissociative identities. Other therapists state that dissociative identity disorder is a coping mechanism used to deal with the trauma of having been severely physically or sexually abused as a child. A child who is being abused and rejected may create a "safe" personality who is not subject to the abuse, or who tries to protect the dominant personality from the abuse. It remains a controversial diagnosis, and many clinical psychologists report never having seen a true case.

Another type of dissociative disorder is that of dissociative amnesia and fugue state: a person forgets some or all of his personal information (amnesia) and may flee to another location (fugue). Dissociative amnesia is usually caused by excessive stress, either because of a major trauma (living through an earthquake) or the cumulative effect of smaller life stresses.

ZAPS: DISSOCIATIVE IDENTITY DISORDER

Questions

1. How easy do you think it would be to fake having dissociative identity disorder? How might a person faking such a disorder be detected?

2. What might be the mechanisms by which an abused child developed several fully formed personalities to reduce anxiety about his or her situation?

3. Why do you think DID is one of the rarest mental illnesses, despite the fact that a high percentage of children are abused and neglected each year?

ZAPS | # Emotional Stroop

How to: This ZAP will work best if you first choose which of the four categories (Spiders, Dirtiness, Crowds, Death) you most fear. Read the instructions and press the **space bar** to continue. Concentrate on the black square on the screen, where the words will appear. As each word appears, press the **r**-key if the word is red, the **g**-key if the word is green, and the **b**-key if the word is blue. Be as quick but as accurate as possible. After each word trial you will receive feedback and the next trial will begin.

You may then perform the modified Stroop task with the other three categories to illustrate that you show an emotional Stroop effect only to the categories for which you have fear, but not to the other categories.

Your best friend is in the passenger seat of your car on the way to a movie. She asks you a question, just as a car from the oncoming traffic swerves into your lane. Your momentary fear (until the oncoming car gets back to its own lane) causes you not to pay attention to your friend's question. Once your heart returns to its normal pace, you ask her to repeat her query.

Why does fear, or any related emotion, distract our attention? Even dangerous stimuli that are not life threatening can cause attention to be directed so that we are unable to process other stimuli taking place at the same time as the danger.

One way to illustrate the effect that even mild fear can have on attention and information processing is through the Emotional Stroop task. The original Stroop task, devised in 1935 by J. Ridley Stroop, presented people with either colored Xs, color words printed in black (such as the word *blue* printed in black ink), or color words printed in a non-corresponding color ink (such as the word *green* printed in red ink). Stroop found that people were slower to name the ink color ink when it was presented in a non-corresponding color word. For example, people were slower to name "red" when they saw the word *green* (printed in red ink) than when they saw *XXXXXX* (also printed in red ink). Stroop hypothesized that people couldn't help but process the word *green*, which distracted them from the ability to produce the word "red" to name the ink color.

The Emotional Stroop uses the same logic; people will be slower to name the color ink of an emotionally tinged word (e.g., the word *snake* written in blue ink) than the ink color of a more neutral word (such as the word *table* printed in blue ink). People's fear of snakes occupies some of their attention when they confront the word *snake*, and it thus takes them longer to identify the color in which the word is written. Someone who likes snakes, but is scared of illness, will be fast to name the ink color of *snake* but slower to name the ink color of *germs*. Fear, after all, is usually specific to a kind of object or situation.

ZAPS: EMOTIONAL STROOP

Questions

1. Can you think of a recent example where you were unable to process information quickly because of stress or pressure?

2. How and why do you think our system is programmed to reduce the processing of information during times of stress? Is this adaptive or not?

3. Some research on memory indicates that a moderate level of stress or adrenaline may improve memories for events (e.g., flashbulb memories). Why does the Emotional Stroop predict worse cognitive performance with material that introduces stress? Do you think the level of stress (high vs. medium vs. low) might explain the difference?

ZAPS | Encoding Specificity

> **How to:** A string of word pairs will appear on the screen, one pair at a time. Try to remember the word pairs as best you can. Afterward, you will be tested on your memory for the words by viewing pairs of words, one of which will appear in capital letters. Place your left index finger on the **c**-key, your right index finger on the m-key. If the capitalized word in each pair of the recognition trials is familiar (you remember it from the learning phase), press the **m**-key. If not, press the c-key.

Jacob is in his bedroom, thinks of something he has to do in the kitchen, but then forgets what he intended to do by the time he reaches the kitchen. To help jog his memory, Jacob returns to the bedroom where he first thought of the task. Sound familiar? Do you get nervous when you have to take an exam in any room other than your classroom? Have you ever passed the waitress from your favorite restaurant but initially didn't recognize her because she was seen in a different context than usual (the sidewalk, rather than inside the restaurant)?

Both you and Jacob have psychological support for wanting to return to the original scene to help recall a single memory or material learned in class. When we learn information, the context in which it is encoded is also encoded, and then can serve as a useful retrieval cue. This is known as the Encoding Specificity Principle—information is best remembered in the same circumstances in which it was learned.

There are several ways that the encoding specificity principle (Tulving) can be instituted.

Physical Context

People can remember information when they re-instate the physical environment in which they first learned it. Usually this means the same room (or even the same desk in a classroom), but need not. Godden and Baddeley (1975) asked scuba divers to suit up and then to listen to a tape recording of 36 unrelated words, either while on dry land or underwater. Half of each encoding group (dry land vs. underwater) stayed in the *same* physical location to recall the word, the other half recalled the words in the *different* physical location (e.g., encoded on dry land/recalled underwater). Subjects allowed both to encode and recall words in the same physical context had better recall.

However, the Same Context effect only held for a recall task; when Godden and Baddeley conducted the same experiment using a recognition task, there was no difference between the Same and Different Context groups. It could be that recognition, being an easier task than recall, doesn't require encoding specificity cues to activate to-be-remembered information.

Experimental Context

Thomson and Tulving (1970) presented subjects with weak-associate word pairs such as *fat-MUTTON*. Subjects were then asked to recall the capitalized word in each pair when either give (a) no cue, (b) the same weakly associated cue ("fat"), or (c) a more strongly associated word (e.g., "leg") than had been presented at time of encoding. Encoding specificity was supported in that the words associated with the target during the learning phase were best at eliciting memory for the target word (even better than words more strongly associated with the target).

The encoding specificity effect is most pronounced for words that had a weak associative pair during the learning phase (e.g., *fat-MUTTON*). When words were paired with a strong associate in the learning phase (e.g., *sting-WASP*), another strongly associated word serves as an equally good retrieval cue (e.g., *bee-WASP*).

State-dependency

Some people have claimed that recalling information is best if you can reinstate the same *internal* state. For instance, if you drink two cups of coffee and then learn a list of words, you'll better recall them a day or so later after also drinking two cups of coffee. State-dependency has uneven support, though, as not all researchers have found evidence to confirm its role in memory.

ZAPS: ENCODING SPECIFICITY

Questions

1. How do you explain the fact that Godden and Baddeley found a physical context effect in the recall task, but not during a recognition task?

2. What do you think is stored along with to-be-remembered information that leads to context effects and state-dependent memory? How does this relate to the notion of retrieval cues, addressed in the "Recalling Information" ZAP demonstration?

ZAPS | False Memory

How to: There are 6 trials in this experiment. In each trial, you will see 12 words that you are to try to remember. A matrix of 12 words will then appear; you are to click on all of the words in this matrix (in any order) that appeared in the previous list. Then move on to the next trial of 12 words.

In the movie, *He Said, She Said,* a romance (and subsequent breakup) is told from the different perspectives of the boyfriend and girlfriend in the film. It highlights the fact that two people can be in the same room, participate in the same event, and yet remember very different things about the event. The movie thus illustrates that our memories are not infallible. This has both good consequences and bad—we will not remember all the bad events of our lives, but we won't remember all the details of the good ones, either.

Where our infallibility of memory may have the most severe consequences is in **eyewitness testimony**. Juries often weigh the testimony of a credible witness over other types of evidence. But what if an eyewitness is wrong? Are they deliberately lying? Is it possible to remember the opposite of what really happened? Or to identify the wrong perpetrator of a crime? When we do misremember an event, what kinds of details are we most likely to get wrong?

This ZAP demonstration is based on work by Underwood (1965). He asked subjects to participate in a **running recognition task**, where each word was presented, one at a time, and subjects simply had to say whether each word had already appeared in the list or not. However, Underwood was able to trick subjects into "recognizing" words that had not been presented, by including a sufficient number of meaningfully related words first. The words *chill, freeze, warm, ice, frigid* would appear (sandwiched between other, non-related words). When the word *cold* would pop up, many subjects reported that *cold* had already appeared in the list. Why? Because the other related words activated a general **schema** about temperature that also activated the word *cold*, thus making them misremember that *cold* was familiar.

Elizabeth Loftus has made a career testing a different way that memories can be altered. In 1974, she (with Palmer) asked students to watch a film of a minor car accident and then answer questions about the film. On the questionnaire, some subjects were asked, "How fast was the car going when it *hit* the other car?" while others were asked, "How fast was the car going when it *smashed* the other car?" Even though all students saw the same film, the speed estimates were significantly higher in the *smashed* group (40.8 mph) than in the *hit* group (31.8 mph). Loftus pointed out that *post-event* information (or *misinformation*) may alter a person's original memory (which may have started out as an accurate memory).

However, the two lines of research—Underwood's and Loftus's—are related: even in studies testing eyewitness testimony, subjects are most likely to misremember details that are consistent with the schema for an event. For example, one week after viewing Loftus and Palmer's accident scene, about a third of the subjects (mis)recalled seeing broken glass (which fits with the schema for an accident). Chances are you couldn't have convinced them that sausages fell out of one of the cars upon impact, since sausages are not consistent with an accident schema. Research shows that eyewitnesses, both in real life and in experiments, are most likely to add in schema-relevant details when they misremember an event. If you want some good news about memory, two thirds of the subjects accurately remembered that there was no broken glass in the accident video.

Name: _____

Class: _____

Professor: _____

Date: _____

ZAPS: FALSE MEMORY

Questions

1. Think back to the last time you had a friendly argument about what happened at a party or a movie? Did you and the other person in the argument differ about critical details of the event or movie? Small details? The general gist of what happened? How does your argument exemplify the points of false memory research?

2. Research shows that eyewitnesses allowed both to return to the scene of a crime or accident *and* to recall all they can without any misleading questions from lawyers or police officers have more accurate memories of the crime/accident. Does Loftus's research predict this?

3. Would children be more or less susceptible to false memories in a running recognition task? A misinformation task involving eyewitness testimony? Explain your answers.

ZAPS | Fan Effect

HOW TO: Press the **Start** button and a sentence will appear that tells the location of a given character (e.g., "The mechanic is at the restaurant."). Study the sentence, then press the Start button to see the next sentence. There will be 8 study sentences altogether. Memorize them as best you can as each sentence appears.

Next, you will be asked to match each character from the sentences to their respective locations. In the third part of this exercise, you will see a series of sentences and must decide (as quickly but as accurately as possible) whether each sentence is true or false.

It's the first day of class. You arrive at your first class in a major lecture hall, and notice a student who looks somewhat befuddled. Being a seasoned student, you ask if he needs help finding his classroom. A relieved smile lights up his face, and you say, "I've had a class in that room before. Follow me." Eager to make conversation, the other student asks, "What class do you have in this lecture hall?" Since you've actually had four classes in this lecture hall over the years, there is a pause before you say "Modern Art." You then mentally run through the list of your previous classes in that building, "Economics 101; U.S. Government; Introduction to Psychology." Why did it take so long to retrieve the information to answer the other student's question? Would you have been faster to respond if you'd had only one class in that lecture hall? Yes, according to the **fan effect**.

One way to conceptualize memory is by a series of connected nodes. Each piece of information or concept we know is connected to all related concepts or facts. For example, we might connect "bird" to "feathers," "nest," "flies," "legs," and so on. However, the more concepts are connected to a concept, the longer it may take to retrieve information. The more distinctive a piece of information, the faster it can be retrieved. If you are asked, "What animals have feathers?" it shouldn't take very long to blurt out, "Birds!" because birds are the only animals with feathers. However, if asked, "What animals have legs?" it will take significantly longer since birds, mammals, amphibians, and reptiles all have legs. The fan effect predicts longer response times to pieces of information that are more highly connected than to distinctive pieces of information.

Within memory research, it has long been known that one of the predominant reasons we have trouble retrieving information is due to interference. For example, if I were to ask what you ordered the last time you visited your favorite Chinese restaurant, all the dishes that you have ordered there over the years would be activated. You would think, "I often order the mu shu pork, the cashew chicken, and the sweet and sour shrimp. But which did I have last time?" However, if asked about your dinner entrée at the fancy restaurant to which your parents took you for parents' weekend, filet mignon would come to mind immediately (because you can't afford to treat yourself to a fancy restaurant and have only been there once). The more distinctive the information (the filet mignon), the easier it is to retrieve.

ZAPS: FAN EFFECT

Questions

1. Construct a spreading activation network about types of familiar and rare birds that you know to illustrate how related concepts are connected to each other.

2. Explain how interference can be instituted within such a spreading activation network to cause the fan effect.

3. Can you think of an explanation as to why you might *not* find the fan effect in research—that retrieval of information should be faster the *more* you know about a topic?

ZAPS | Feature Net

> **HOW TO:** You will be "training" the program to recognize letters within words by continually presenting letters to the program. In many cases, the letters are only partially depicted, or some features of each letter are missing.
>
> You may choose a word or single letter from a list, or type in a 4-letter word yourself. You may also choose whether the word will appear for a short or long duration. Press **Start** to begin each experiment, and to see how the feature net first matches features, then recognizes letters based, in part, on bigram knowledge.

Your best friend is notorious for bad handwriting, but you have no trouble reading her notes. Why is it that you can recognize your friend's handwriting but few other people can? And how do pharmacists recognize the scrawl of doctors on prescription orders?

Some ability to recognize letters and words is based on familiarity; since you see your friend's handwriting more often on notes, you will have an easier time deciphering her letters and words than will a stranger. Likewise, pharmacists are used to seeing physicians' handwriting, and thus recognize prescribed drugs and dosages more accurately than patients. In addition, familiarity with individual words can influence how quickly and accurately we recognize words and letters. In other words, **word frequency** affects recognition processes. Highly familiar or frequent words are recognized faster than rare words with lower frequencies. Pharmacists know the names of drugs much better than laypeople and can thus decipher written prescriptions because of their pharmacy expertise.

Computer scientists have been interested in designing programs that can learn to recognize letters, even under conditions of uncertainty (such as low lighting, missing features). One of the most effective programs is known as a **feature net**. It assumes that letters and words are processed through a series of temporal stages—the program first detects individual features of letters, then pieces those features together to identify letters. Combinations of letters then permit recognition of words.

Sometimes, though, we can recognize even misspelled words, or (like our friend's handwriting) words in which two letters are blurred together. How does this happen? As you saw in the Word Superiority Effect ZAP, past knowledge about words and their construction can facilitate our ability to recognize the individual letters within a word (even if only partial information is available about individual letters). In some feature nets, the program is able to tabulate and store information about common letter pairs, known as **bigrams**. For example, *sh, ea, -le* are frequent letter pairs. Thus if you see the letter *s* followed by a letter that is unclear, there is a high probability in English words that the second letter is an *h*, given your bigram knowledge. Remembering combinations of frequent letters improves our accurate detection, even when information is incomplete.

Name: _____

Class: _____

Professor: _____

Date: _____

ZAPS: FEATURE NET

Questions

1. How similar is the training that people undergo when they are learning to read and recognize letters to the training that you gave the computer?

2. Why does knowledge of the frequency of letter pairs (bigrams) within a language help recognize letters with missing information? What would happen if information about bigrams was taken out of the program?

3. In the days before spell-check features in word processing programs, people were told to read a paper backward to check for spelling errors. Why would this have led to better detection of errors than reading the paper forward?

> **How to:** You will be presented with a schematic diagram of the different nerve fibers responsible for carrying pain and non-pain messages to different areas of the brain, such as the motor cortex, limbic system, somatosensory cortex, etc. This diagram also contains parts for the inhibitory and transmission neurons, which form the "gateway" for the delivery of pain messages. Four stimuli (e.g., **inject morphine**) appear above the diagram; click on one to see how it is carried out by the neurons. You may then click on various elements of the schematic diagram to find out more about the role each part plays in the system. When you are ready, click on the button beneath the diagram to see what happens when the stimulus you have chosen is introduced into the system.
>
> The **main menu** button will take you back to the beginning and let you choose another of the 4 stimuli.

Have you ever sprained your ankle or pulled a muscle and rubbed the area to make it feel better? Why does that work? In fact, you might predict that rubbing a part of your body that is pain would intensify the pain, but it doesn't. Melzack and Wall (1965) wrote a revolutionary paper that explained why things such as rubbing sprained ankles, immersing yourself in a hot bath to ease muscle aches, applying an ice pack to a sprain, and acupuncture actually reduce feelings of pain. The theory they proposed was called the Gate Control Theory of pain.

When part of your body is damaged, such as an ankle, a muscle, or even an appendix, pain messages are sent via the spinal column, through the thalamus, to parts of the cerebral cortex. These pain messages are conducted along small diameter nerve fibers (called **C fibers**), which are not myelinated (i.e., they do not contain a fatty myelin sheath around their axons).

Information about touch and pressure, where parts of your body are in space (called **proprioception**), however, are sent along large-diameter nerves (called **A-beta fibers**), which *are* myelinated. Why does this make a difference? Myelinated neurons can send messages faster along greater distances because of a process called **saltatory conduction**. When myelinated neurons conduct a message down their axon, it is analogous to throwing a ball from person to person across a gym; unmyelinated axons conduct that same message by "handing" the ball (or message) from one person to another in a continuous line. Obviously, throwing the ball relay-style will conduct the message more quickly.

The second point of the Gate Control Theory is that there are certain hypothetical "gates" in the spinal cord and thalamus where it is determined whether a message will get passed on or not. At these gates, the faster, large-diameter neurons (A-beta fibers) can inhibit the messages from the medium-diameter **A-delta fibers** (which transmit sharp, immediate pains, such as burning yourself on a hot stove) and the smaller C fibers (containing messages about diffuse, throbbing pain that lasts after the initial body damage). Thus, when you rub a sprained ankle, the sensory messages of touch travel faster along the A-beta fibers than the pain messages travel along the A-delta and C fibers. The messages of touch will reach the "gate" first and thus get through to the brain, while the pain messages will be inhibited.

At a chemical level, the excitatory pain connections cause the release of **substance P**, the neurotransmitter responsible for pain messages. Inhibitory connections cause the release of **endorphins** (short for **endogenous morphines**)—the body's natural pain killer. It is thought that pain relief from acupuncture, and the "runner's high" reported by some athletes, is due to the release of endorphins.

The Gate Control Theory of pain has had profound clinical applications for people suffering from chronic or acute pain. For instance, many women in labor report that taking a hot bath reduced or eliminated the pain of contractions. A system known as TENS (for transcutaneous electrical nerve stimulation) sends pulses of electrical stimulation through electrodes placed on an area of pain to greatly reduce the perception of pain. It has been used successfully with people suffering from lower-back pain, whiplash, carpal tunnel syndrome, athletic injuries, and labor pain.

ZAPS: GATE CONTROL THEORY

Questions

1. What have you found to be effective techniques for reducing pain after an injury? Can any of these techniques be explained by the Gate Control Theory?

2. Do you think that massaging a wound interferes with the sensation of pain (its detection) or with it perception (recognizing a feeling as painful)? Use the neurological information above to explain and justify your answer.

How to: The Discovery section of this ZAP is designed to acquaint you with genetic transmission of eye color. BROWN is a dominant trait and BLUE is a recessive trait. On each trial, you will see a picture of a mother and a father, with 4 children underneath. Press on the buttons underneath the mother and father to change their genes, and then to see how the possible inheritance of their children changes.

In the Experience section, you will be shown a mother and a father and their genotypes. You must first predict the genotype of each of 4 hypothetical children by clicking on the gray button beneath each child until you have the correct combination of genes. Secondly, you must judge whether each child's genotype means that he or she is ill, healthy, or a carrier for a given disease. Your judgments will be based on whether the disease is Autosomal dominant, Autosomal recessive, X-linked dominant, or X-linked recessive. Drag the correct diagnosis ("healthy," "ill," or "carrier") to each child. After you have made the judgments for all four children, click the **Check** button to see if you are correct. You will have up to 3 attempts to get each problem correct.

Can you roll your tongue into a cylinder? Believe it or not, whether you have this ability or not is based on your genes. What is your blood type? Are you Rh positive or negative? Tall or short? Blue-eyed, brown-eyed, or green-eyed? Allergic to poison ivy? Are you extroverted or introverted? Good at math or language? All these traits—physical, psychological, behavioral—are known to be genetically influenced.

The expression of our genetic inheritance for a given trait is called our **phenotype**. The combination of genes we have inherited that influence or determine that trait is called our **genotype**. For example, Sarah and Jamal both have brown eyes. Their phenotype, thus, is the same. However, Sarah inherited two brown-eyed genes (one from each parent), while Jamal inherited one brown-eyed gene and one blue-eyed gene. The genotypes for Sarah and Jamal are different, even though they have the same eye color. The different *versions* of a gene for a given trait (e.g., blue-eye gene; brown-eye gene; green-eye gene) are called **alleles**.

Some of our traits we can see in our parents, others may be evident in our grandparents (but skipped our parents). It seems easy to see how our parents could pass on physical or behavioral characteristics to us, but how could traits from our grandparents skip a generation? This is because the genetic transmission of traits is not identical for all genes. Some traits, such as having Type A or Type B blood, are **dominant**. That is, they "beat out" other versions of genes for blood type. Type O blood is **recessive**—it is beat out by Type A or B blood genes. The only way to have Type O blood is to inherit two O-genes. Some traits, however, are **co-dominant**—a person who inherits a Type A blood gene from one parent, and a Type B blood gene from the other parent, will have type AB blood. Furthermore, not all traits are due to a single gene. Many of our traits—height, intelligence—are probably influenced by multiple genes, and also by diet and environmental factors.

Humans have 46 chromosomes, which are broken down into 23 pairs. One chromosome in each pair was inherited from a person's mother, the other from their father. Of those 23 pairs of chromosomes, 22 are known as **autosomes**. The other pair is the **sex chromosomes** because that pair is responsible for whether we are male or female. Most of our genetic information is found on the autosomes (after all, there are 22 pairs of those compared to 1 pair of sex chromosomes). Some of the traits specified by genes on the autosomes are dominant, others are recessive, and some are co-dominant. Traits on the sex chromosomes (the **X** and the **Y chromosome**) can also be dominant or recessive, but transmission of traits on the sex chromosomes is determined by a person's sex.

All children inherit one of their mother's X chromosomes. Females inherit an X from their father; males inherit a Y chromosome from their father. The X-chromosome is larger than the Y, and thus carries more genetic information. Most of the X-linked traits that have been studied are recessive. Red-green color blindness, hemophilia, and Duchenne muscular dystrophy are all examples of X-linked, recessive traits. All 3 affect males more than females. But how, you ask? After all, females have twice the probability of inheriting genes for these disorders, since they have 2 X-chromosomes. Recall, though, that these recessive traits mean that females would have to inherit the gene for, say, red-green color blindness from *both* parents to phenotypically express the trait. A female with just 1 allele for red-green color blindness can pass on that gene to her offspring, so she is said to be a **carrier**. Males, on the other hand, will express an X-linked recessive trait because they have no corresponding "healthy" X-chromosome to overrule the gene for the recessive disorder (remember that the Y-chromosome is smaller, with less genetic information).

This ZAP gives you more information on each type of genetic inheritance, and examples of autosomal and X-linked dominant and recessive traits.

ZAPS: GENETICS

Questions

1. Construct a family tree of eye color for your own family (or a family you know well who has a variety of eye colors). Try to get information for at least 3 generations. Can you figure out the genotypes for each family member?

2. Which traits that you exhibit are dominant? Recessive? Autosomal or dominant? Do you know anyone who has a genetic disorder? What is the history of that trait within the person's family?

3. If it were possible, would you be willing to try for a "designer baby" that had the hair and eye color, intelligence, abilities, and personality you deemed optimum?

Gestalt Problem Solving

HOW TO: A balance scale and 8 coins will appear on the screen. Your task is to identify which of the 8 is false (and weighs less than the others). Drag coins to each side of the balance scale and then press **Check** to see the effect on the balance scale (whether it tilts to one side or the other, or stays even). Drag the coins off the balance scale and repeat the process until you figure out which is the false coin. If you think you have the correct answer, drag the potentially false coin to the **drop false coin here** box on the right side of the screen.

However, on each trial you may only use the **Check** button twice. If you are unable to figure out which is the false coin, press the **Restart** button to begin the process again (a new coin will become the false coin).

In 1784, when 7-year-old German student Carl Friedrich Gauss was asked to determine the sum of the integers from 1 to 100, his hand shot up with the correct answer much faster than any of his classmates. When his teacher expressed skepticism that he could calculate that quickly, young Gauss pointed out that the sum of the numbers 1 to 100 was simply 50 pairs of 101 (1 + 100; 2 + 99; 3 + 98 . . .). The Gestaltists, a group of German psychologists in the late 1800s–1900s, said that young Gauss's ability to see the elegant solution that eluded his classmates was due to a flash of "insight." In other words, while the other students began computing the answer, Gauss saw a pattern that helped him solve the mathematics problem in a new way.

The Gestaltists argued that the best problem solving involved **cognitive restructuring**, in which a problem is seen in a novel way. When one can see new arrangements or patterns, it may lead to creative solutions and flashes of insight. Continuing to view a problem in old, nonproductive ways, or to continue to use the same strategies (as did Gauss's classmates), is known as **fixation**.

It is not that Gauss's classmates were being illogical; after all, their solution would have resulted in a correct answer eventually. However, computing the sum of the consecutive integers 1 to 100 longhand lacks the elegance and creativity for which we admire Gauss's brilliance. The Gestaltists emphasized that truly creative problem solving may involve thinking outside the box to detect novel solutions.

There are 2 main types of fixation that prevent effective problem solving. The first is adopting a **mental set**, meaning that we continue to use the same tired problem-solving strategies that we have tried in the past. Sometimes, old strategies may help us to arrive at an answer (after all, Gauss's classmates who had begun adding the integers from 1 to 100 would eventually have computed 5,050). However, these strategies from the past may not be the best, most creative, or most efficient way to solve a problem. The second type of fixation is **functional fixedness**, when a person only sees the standard use for an object. For example, imagine a father who laments that the bath leaks every time someone takes a shower, and thinks, "I have to re-caulk that bathtub soon." Three days later, he is still lamenting because he didn't realize that his son's Play Doh could have been used as a temporary measure to prevent water from leaking into the wall. Why couldn't the father see this creative solution? He could only think of Play Doh as a "toy," and thus was prevented from seeing its home repair function.

ZAPS: GESTALT PROBLEM SOLVING

Questions

1. Think of one or two examples from the past when you (or someone you know) exhibited fixation. How did you resolve the fixation?

2. Why do you think we are so dependent on familiar ways of problem solving, and so unlikely to think creatively in problem-solving situations?

3. Think of seven new uses for a paper clip.

How to: On each trial, a 3×3 matrix will appear. Focus on the matrix, in which 9 letters will appear briefly and then disappear. Shortly thereafter, a > sign will be presented next to one of the three rows in the matrix (upper, middle, or lower). Type in the letters that appeared in that row as accurately as possible, from left to right. Once you type a letter into a cell, the cursor will automatically jump to the next cell (and you will not be able to change answers in previous cells). There will be 5 practice trials, followed by 36 real trials.

Everyone is familiar with continuing to "see" a white flash after someone has taken their photograph. And have you ever asked someone to repeat something they've just said, only to say, "Never mind," as you process the initial sentence? Or continued to grimace from an unpleasant taste, even though you've already swallowed? If so, you're already familiar with **sensory memory**. In any sensory modality—vision, hearing, taste, and so on—stimuli seem to be maintained for a brief time after they have disappeared.

In hearing, sensory memory is referred to as **echoic memory** (just as a phrase you shout into a cave lingers momentarily). In vision, sensory memory is called **iconic memory**, as a visual icon is what lingers. The Partial Report procedure developed by Sperling (1960) tests iconic memory.

In a Full Report procedure, subjects presented with a 9-item matrix can typically recall an average of 4.5 items (50%) after the matrix has disappeared. Sperling argued that this was indicative of their *memory* for the matrix rather than an accurate perception of the matrix. He assumed that subjects momentarily have a full image of the letters in the matrix, but that the image fades as they start to report the letters. The **Partial Report procedure** is a way to compensate for the "fading" of the image. A person looks at a matrix of letters but then is asked only to report the letters in one row (without knowing which row will be tested until the letters disappear). Subjects can often recall an average of 75% of the letters in a single row (equivalent to visually remembering 7 items out of a 9-item matrix). Sperling argued that if accuracy is higher in the Partial Report than in the Full Report procedure, this is evidence that people initially maintain the entire matrix in their sensory memory.

A related issue is how long iconic memory lasts. Echoic memory has been claimed to last about 2 to 3 seconds, but iconic memory lasts only 1/3 of a second. Sperling and others have found that subjects have an advantage in the Partial Report procedure only up to 1/3 of a second. If the cue about which row to report (upper, middle, lower) is delayed longer than 1/3 of a second, performance drops to the same level as the Full Report.

ZAPS: ICONIC MEMORY

Questions

1. Think of an example of how a stimulus seems to be maintained in each of the sensory modalities: vision, hearing, touch, taste, smell.

2. What might be the purpose of why we evolved the ability to hold sensory information briefly in a sensory memory? When is such an ability useful?

| Implicit Learning

> **How to:** You will see 4 connected squares on the screen. Circles then appear in each of the 4 squares. Important: Place your left index and middle fingers on the **c**-key and **x**-key, respectively. Place your right index and middle fingers on the **m**-key and **comma**-key, respectively. These keys correspond to the 4 squares located on the screen. As the sequence of circles appears, press the **x**-key whenever a circle appears in the left-most square; the **c**-key when it appears in the inner left square; the **m**-key if the circle is in the right inner square; and the **comma**-key when it is in the right-most square. Respond as quickly, but as accurately, as possible.
>
> Trials are presented in 12 blocks of 24. You may take a short break after each block, and then press the **space bar** to continue. Your data will be presented at the end.

Pretend you are opening a door with a key. Did you turn the key to the right to "open" the door? How did you know to turn a key to the right to open a lock? Did you ever deliberately sit down and memorize this rule?

And did someone tell you that riding a bike up a steep hill is easier if you stand up to pedal, or did you somehow just know it?

Sometimes we learn the basic requirements or rules of a task without ever formally studying those rules or even being able to articulate them. This seemingly automatic, and perhaps unconscious, rule learning is called **implicit learning**, and is measured by the improvement in performance that we show as we practice a task. One of the ways to test implicit learning in the laboratory is through a **serial reaction-time task**: a person is given a task to perform a series of actions (hence serial), and they get faster and faster at the exercise (reaction-time) without ever being told the principles or guidelines for the task.

Amnesic patients sometimes show implicit learning in problem-solving tasks, such as the **Tower of Hanoi problem**. This is true even when the amnesic doesn't remember ever having seen the Tower of Hanoi problem before. This is an easy problem to try yourself: First, draw 3 circles side by side on a piece of paper. On the left-most circle, stack 3 or 5 coins of varying sizes, from largest to smallest. For example, you could stack a quarter, then a nickel, then a dime. The problem asks you to reassemble this stack on the right-most circle in as few moves as possible, with the following caveats: (1) only 1 coin at a time can be moved; and (2) a larger coin can never rest on top of a smaller coin.

Try this exercise with 3 coins before reading its explanation below. Then try it again with 4 coins, and count your number of moves in each case.

The "rule" behind solving the Tower of Hanoi problem in a minimal number of moves has to do with where you move the first coin. When the number of coins you use is an odd number (3, 5, 7 . . .), the top coin must be moved to the right-most circle to accomplish the least number of moves (using 3 coins, you will need a minimum of 7 moves to solve the problem). If, on the other hand, you use an even number of coins (e.g., 4), the top coin should first be moved to the middle circle to minimize the number of moves toward the solution.

Anterograde amnesic patients, who have trouble remembering any new factual or episodic information, nevertheless show improvement in the strategy for Tower of Hanoi solutions. Even though they report not having participated in the Tower of Hanoi task, and don't remember the experimenter who tests them (even after multiple experimental sessions), they nevertheless get more adept and faster at minimizing the number of moves for solution. They implicitly learn to adapt their first move based on the number of coins or disks in the initial pile, but are never consciously aware of improving, or of the heuristic that they are using.

ZAPS: IMPLICIT LEARNING

Questions

1. What types of skills have you learned implicitly? What has happened to your accuracy and speed in performing those skills or tasks?

2. Do you think that improvement in implicit learning tasks such as the serial reaction-time task in the ZAP is due to cognitive factors (learning a rule), or to getting faster at carrying out the motor component of the task (pressing the keys that correspond to the circles as they appear)? Explain. It is worthwhile to test this by performing the ZAP experiment again, this time reversing your hands so that the x- and c-keys are pressed by your right hand, and the m- and comma-keys are pressed by your left hand. (Then see the explanation for what this tests in the "Theory" section of the ZAP.)

ZAPS | Lateral Inhibition

How to: There are 2 parts to the Discovery section of this ZAP. Part I contains 5 assignments; Part II contains 6 assignments. Per assignment, press the **Start** key to begin. Based on the excitatory and inhibitory connections among the neurons depicted, figure out the firing rate for each neuron. After completing each assignment, press the **Check** key for feedback as to whether you are correct. When all your answers are correct, press **Next** to proceed to the next assignment.

Is what we see an accurate depiction of the world? When we perceive "red," is there really a red object in front of us? And when we perceive motion, is there really something moving? For the most part, our visual system quickly and accurately picks out shape, color, motion. There are occasions, however, in which we perceive things inaccurately, sometimes because of the circumstances in which objects are perceived. For example, a bright green sweater does not appear quite as bright under low lighting conditions (even though we know it has not changed color).

There are characteristics of our visual system that may alter the way we see or perceive stimuli. One such characteristic is the **lateral inhibition** that takes place in the neurons of the retina. Neurons convey information to other neurons and the brain by communicating with each other in complex transactions. Oftentimes, the connections among neurons are excitatory— that is, one message sends a message to a second neuron that increases the likelihood that the second neuron will have an action potential, and will continue to pass on the message. In other cases, the communication from neuron 1 to neuron 2 is *inhibitory*; neuron 1 decreases the likelihood of an action potential in neuron 2. "Lateral" means "to the side" and refers to the inhibition that takes place between neurons in the retina that are side by side.

In vision, the higher the rate at which a neuron fires, the more "light" we will perceive. The lower the rate at which a neuron fires, the more "dark" we will perceive. Thus, if a neuron that *should* respond to light/white is inhibited by its neighbors, it will send a darker message, tricking us into thinking we see grey or darker regions. This explains an illusion known as the Hermann Grid (see ZAPS experiment online). When we look at a full Hermann Grid, we perceive spots of gray at all the A intersections. Why? And why don't we perceive gray spots at the B spots?

Even though the B spots are bounded by 2 black regions, and thus receive some inhibition, they do not receive as much inhibition as spot A, which is bounded by 4 black regions. Thus, the gray spots appear at A, but not at B.

ZAPS: LATERAL INHIBITION

Questions

1. What might be the benefits to lateral inhibition in detecting objects and stimuli in the real world?

2. Why might inhibitory processes among neurons have evolved? Can you think of circumstances in which *not* passing on a message would be adaptive?

3. Try to invent a new visual illusion that relies on lateral inhibition.

Lexical Decision Task

> **How to:** Keep your eyes focused on the middle of the screen, and keep your index fingers on the **m**-key and the **c**-key. A word or letter string (that does not form a word, e.g., *thexe*) will appear. Press the **m**-key if the stimulus is a real word; press the **c**-key if the stimulus is not a real word.
>
> A second word or nonsense word will appear just below the first stimulus. Judge whether the second stimulus is a word (**m**-key) or a nonsense word (**c**-key). Be as fast but as accurate as you can be. There are 45 trials in all; each trial will appear automatically after you respond.

Imagine that you are handed a pile of papers on which are listed every word in your vocabulary and its meaning—your **mental lexicon** in paper form. Your task is to organize the vocabulary words in a file cabinet so that you could always find them when you needed them. How would you organize the words? Alphabetically? By grammatical class—with nouns, verbs, and adjectives in separate drawers? Or by meaning—living things in one file drawer, nonliving things in another, mathematical terms in a third?

The Lexical Decision Task (LDT) is one of many ways that psychologists use to assess how our lexicon, or mental dictionary, is organized. The LDT requires that subjects make judgments about whether a string of letters presented visually is a legal word or not. Because educated adults are unlikely to make errors in this task, the main measurement of interest is response time—how long subjects take to decide whether a letter string is a word or nonword.

Psychologists can then tease apart the factors that influence reaction time to words: Is the number of syllables important? What about word frequency— are common words (*religion*) recognized more quickly than low-frequency words (*esophagus*)? Are words with regular spellings (*cape*) more easily recognized than words with irregular phonetic spellings (*yacht*), indicating that there is phonological mediation in word recognition?

Frequency turns out to be an important factor in word recognition; high-frequency words are recognized more quickly than low-frequency words. But why? Imagine each word has its own **threshold**, which determines the level of activation required to "light up" that word in a recognition task. Because of greater exposure to common, high-frequency words, the threshold for those words is lower. It takes less activation and less time to light up those words, resulting in faster reaction times. This is analogous to being able to retrieve the names of your family members more quickly than the names of your neighbors, or the names of your favorite movie stars more quickly than the names of the minor character actors who played in the same movies.

Lexical Decision Tasks are also a good way to find out about how the mental lexicon is structured. One robust effect is that of **priming**. In one experiment, the word *circus* is presented in one trial and it takes a person 600 milliseconds to judge that it is a word. Another letter string is presented, then the word *circus* again. It is likely that the second time the person sees *circus*, it may only take 550 msec to respond; this is known as **repetition priming**. Or, imagine *circus* is presented, then a word with an associated meaning, like *trapeze*. *Trapeze* will be recognized faster than if *circus* had not appeared just before it. In other words, *circus* sparked **semantic priming** of the related word *trapeze*. What this tells the researcher is that *circus* and *trapeze* are somehow connected in that person's mental lexicon.

How can we explain these priming effects? In the case of repetition priming, activation of *circus* after the first presentation takes a while to fade. Thus, when *circus* is presented again quickly, some of the activation still remains, and it takes less time for its threshold to be achieved the second time. With semantic priming, it is assumed that words related in meaning are connected to each other; when one is activated, its charge spreads to connected words. If one of those connected words (*trapeze*) is presented shortly after the first (*circus*), *trapeze* will still have some residual activation, and will thus take less time to recognize. The degree of **spreading activation** will be based on how closely the two words are associated in meaning. *Popcorn* might be sold at circuses, but is less closely related than is *trapeze*, and thus would not receive the same facilitation from spreading activation.

Some of the other ways that psychologists might use to test the organization of the lexicon are by analyzing speech errors (especially word substitutions people make), and word retrieval (as in tip-of-the-tongue experience).

ZAPS: LEXICAL DECISION TASK

Questions

1. How might spreading activation actually *in*crease speech errors and tip-of-the-tongue experiences? Would you expect speech errors and tip-of-the-tongue experiences to be more common with high-frequency words or with low-frequency words? Why?

2. Do you think semantic relatedness is the sole criterion that influences spreading activation? For example, would one noun be more likely to reduce the lexical decision time for another noun, or for an equally associated verb? Explain your reasoning.

> **HOW TO:** After pressing the **Start** button, read each of the 25 sentences aloud and try to feel the mood induced by each. A list of words to remember will then appear. After a short game, you will be asked to engage in 2 memory tasks for the words.

Your roommate takes one of your TV dinners . . . again. A black cloud settles over you, and every transgression of your roommate from the entire semester comes flooding back ("That's the third time he stole my frozen dinner. . . . And what about playing that awful music every evening . . . to top it all off, he lost the sweatshirt I loaned him . . .)—5 minutes before, you may have greeted your roommate warmly and asked about his classes. As soon as the prospect of having no dinner occurs, your attitude toward your roommate and your personal memories of him shift from good to bad.

Memory researchers have long known that situational factors when one learns a piece of information can provide great retrieval cues for that information later. The **encoding specificity effect** claims that memory will be best when encoding and memory situations match up (see the Encoding Specificity ZAP for another illustration of the effect). In this ZAP, the "situation" involves the match-up of mood and the kind of material one is learning. This is known as the **mood congruency effect**. You will tend to remember negative emotionally tinged words best when in a negative mood.

In contrast, the example from the first paragraph illustrates a related phenomenon—the **mood dependency effect**—in which we tend to retrieve information best if in the same mood as when we first learned the information. Each time in the past that your roommate stole your TV dinner, or played distasteful music, or lost your sweatshirt, probably led you to be in a dark mood. Thus, the next time you're in a dark mood because he takes your frozen dinner (for the third time!), all the previous bad-mood episodes are remembered. The **mood dependency effect** also predicts that if your roommate takes you out to dinner (to compensate for having eaten your frozen dinner), you will better remember all the great times you've had with your roommate from the past.

ZAPS: MEMORY BIAS

Questions

1. What is the most recent personal example you can think of that illustrates the mood congruency memory bias effect? Do you think mood congruency is an automatic memory bias, or could you deliberately alter the kinds of information you retrieve when happy or sad?

2. Construct a theoretical explanation involving memory encoding and retrieval to explain the mood congruency effect.

3. In your opinion, how specific is the mood congruency effect? Does it only work for happy versus sad moods, or would you tend to retrieve angry memories when angry, silly moments from the past when silly, bored memories when bored?

How TO: On each trial, you will be presented with a number of items (either digits, letters, or words), one at a time. Try to remember these items in order. A matrix with 9 items will appear; click on the items that you saw, in order. Once you have made a choice, it cannot be changed. Press the **Next** button to start the next trial. There are 3 practice trials, followed by 25 test trials.

Raise your hand if you have used up *all* your long-term memory and can't possibly learn one more fact. Not even the most educated of your friends could claim to have used up all his or her long-term memory capacity. And a good thing, too, or the money you are paying for college tuition would all be for naught. Most of us, though, are all too aware that we have a **limited capacity** for short-term memory (STM). If we are driving past the supermarket, and think of 4 items we need to stop and buy, we simply remember them. If we have 10 items, we write them down on a shopping list.

Atkinson and Shiffrin's (1971) **Multistore Model** of memory claims that there are 3 separate stores (or holding rooms) for memory: sensory store, short-term memory, and long-term memory. Each of these differs in its **duration** (how long information can be held), its **code** (the form that information is held in—whether visual, verbal/acoustic, semantic), and its **capacity** (how much information can be held). The Memory Span procedure tests for the capacity of STM. George Miller (1956) reviewed many research articles on STM and claimed that the number 7 kept popping up as the average number of items that people could maintain in STM. He called it "the Magic Number 7," but claimed that people have an average **range** of 5–9 items that they can keep in mind, so the range of STM is considered to be 7 ± 2.

But imagine you were given the following list to remember: *pool, cookie, little, car, league, chip, swimming, chocolate, wash, baseball.* That is a list of 10 words, which exceeds the hypothesized limit of STM. Did you notice connections among the words that might facilitate your memory? If so, you engaged in **chunking**—the combination of smaller pieces of information into larger, meaningful units. What if you were given the words as: *swimming pool, chocolate chip cookie, little league baseball,* and *car wash?* That's 10 words, but only 4 phrases.

So what counts as an "item" in Miller's Magic Number 7? Each of the 4 phrases would count as 1 item in Miller's 7 ± 2 range, because the phrases form meaningful units. Chunking items can seem to expand the limited capacity of STM—not because you've really expanded STM beyond the average of 7 items, but because you've made the items larger units. This also works for visual STM. DeGroot (1965, 1966) discovered that chess masters exhibited better STM for where chess pieces were located in a game because of their ability to create meaningful "chunks" of chess pieces (based on their expertise). However, the items to-be-remembered can only increase moderately—Simon (1974) fell within the 7 ± 2 range up for 1-syllable, 2-syllable, and 3-syllable words, but fell to a memory span of 4 when he tested himself with 2-word phrases.

Another finding is that the capacity of STM is dependent on what kind of material you are trying to remember. People tend to have the longest digit span (memory span for numbers), followed by colors, letters, words, and geometric shapes. Random shapes and nonsense syllables yield the shortest memory span (between 3 and 4, rather than the standard 7 ± 2; Cavanagh, 1972). Thus, information that is meaningful, such as numbers, letters, and words, leads to longer short-term memory spans than nonmeaningful information, such as nonsense syllables or random shapes.

It appears that nature has provided us with a limited short-term memory span, but that we do have strategies at hand to help "expand" our STM capacity.

ZAPS: MEMORY SPAN

Questions

1. Should there be a difference between your ability to remember a sequence of English words versus your memory span for a list of unfamiliar words in Swahili? Why? What is the best explanation for why meaningful material is better remembered in STM than nonmeaningful material?

2. Why should using digits (numbers) typically yield the largest memory span, over that of letters, words, or nonsense syllables? How could you get the memory span for words or letters to equal that of numbers? What strategies can help a person improve his or her memory span?

3. How does one's memory span influence performance on the serial position effect? (See associated ZAP.)

ZAPS | Memory Span

> **How to:** Focus on the middle of the screen. Two letter Fs will appear, usually in different orientations. Your task is to press the **m**-key if the 2 figures are the same (but in different orientations), and to press the **c**-key if the 2 figures are mirror images of each other. Be sure to keep your right index finger on the **m**-key and your left index finger on the **c**-key. You will be given feedback about whether you are correct or not, and the next trial will begin in a few seconds. There will be 3 practice trials, then 48 real trials.

Time how long it takes you to read a paragraph in a textbook right side up, and then how long it takes you to read the same paragraph upside down. Why does it take longer to read upside down? One possibility is that, since words are easier to recognize right side up, you were mentally rotating the letters and/or words as you read. Although this is effective because you are then able to recognize the upside-down words, it adds time to your reading.

Some of the earliest experiments in 2-dimensional rotation were conducted with capital letters. Cooper and Shepard (1973) asked subjects to decide whether a letter was either in correct formation (R), or a mirror image of itself (Я). In addition, the letters could be rotated 60, 120, 180, 240, or 300 degrees from upright position. Subjects' judgment times were highest for the 180-degree rotation letters, second highest for the 60- and 300-degree rotations, and third highest for the 120- and 240-degree rotations. The stimuli in upright positions (0 rotation) were responded to most quickly.

The greater the distance the subjects had to rotate the letters in order to judge whether they were correct or mirror images, the longer it took them. However, people could rotate their image clockwise to upright position, or counterclockwise, since the times for 60 degrees (counterclockwise rotation) and 300 degrees (clockwise rotation) were the same.

Cooper (1975) used 2-dimensional nonsense shapes (called **polygons**) and confirmed that judgment times as to whether 2 figures were the same or different was based on differences in the angle. The more one figure had to be rotated to compare to the other, the longer the reaction times (RT). Furthermore, Cooper (1975) found that RT was not dependent on whether the polygons were simple or complex, but only on the angle of rotation. This illustrates that people were not performing a point-by-point comparison to decide if 2 polygons were the same or not (if they had been, the complex polygons with more points would have led to longer response times).

Such findings have led researchers to claim that our visual system not only has mechanisms for identification or recognition of familiar patterns (such as letters), but also mechanisms for transforming those patterns (e.g., rotation processes).

ZAPS: MENTAL ROTATION, 2-D

Questions

1. Look at photos from different angles—sideways, upside down, at a
   45-degree angle. Are you cognizant of mentally rotating the images
   in order to recognize the scene or face in the photos? Does it matter
   if the photo is one that is familiar to you or not?

2. Most visual stimuli—letters, objects, faces—have a standard orientation. Thus, it makes sense for our visual system to mentally turn them
   upright when we see them at different angles to better match them
   to our representations in memory of those stimuli. How many expo-
   sures to a face or letters do you think it would take to recognize
   upside-down items *without* having to rotate them?

ZAPS | Mental Rotation, 3-D

> **HOW TO:** Focus on the middle of the screen. Two figures will
> appear, usually in different orientations. Your task is to press the
> **m**-key if the 2 figures are the same (but in different orientations)
> and the **c**-key if the 2 figures are mirror images of each other.
> Be sure to keep your right index finger on the **m**-key and your
> left index finger on the **c**-key. You will be given feedback about
> whether you are correct or not, and the next trial will begin in
> a few seconds. There will be 5 practice trials, then 48 real trials.

How many windows are on the bottom floor of the house in which you grew
up? (Write down your answer and check the next time you visit your parents.)
How were you able to answer that question? Were you cognizant of using a
mental image of your house? Did you mentally "walk around" the house in
your image, or did you stand in one "place" and rotate the house on its axis?

Your house is obviously a 3-dimensional object, and you probably represented it as 3-dimensional in your image. If you walked around your imaginal
house, this is similar to mental scanning (see the next ZAP); if you rotated
your house, this is similar to the 3-dimensional rotation addressed in this ZAP.

Shepard and Metzler (1971) presented subjects with pairs of line drawings representing 3-dimensional block figures (you may remember these
from the PSATs you took in high school). Subjects had to decide whether the
2 figures depicted the same figure or different figures. The 2 were either
identical in orientation, rotated within a given plane (2-dimensionally) or
rotated 3-dimensionally. In both the plane and 3-D rotations, response time
increased as the angle of rotation increased. Furthermore, there was only
a minimal difference between the plane and 3-D rotations. Shepard and
Metzler explained that subjects must have been using mental rotation to
decide whether the 2 figures in each trial were the same or different—the

longer the angle of rotation, the longer the RT (reaction time). As with the studies on 2-D rotations of letters discussed in the previous ZAP, there was a linear relationship between rotation angle and RT.

These findings are analogous to what would happen if we held 3-D figures and rotated one of them to see if it matched the other in real space. Finke (1989) claimed that both image and physical transformations are governed by the same laws of motion. He laid out 5 principles of mental imagery, the fourth of which is that visual imagery has **transformational equivalence** with rotating items in real space. Just as it would take us longer to rotate an object 180 degrees than it would to rotate it 30 degrees, so, too, it takes longer to visually rotate an image 180 degrees (over 30).

ZAPS: MENTAL ROTATION, 3-D

Questions

1. Would you have expected 3-D rotation to take longer than 2-D rotation? Why didn't Shepard and Metzler find this? Why do these findings support the claim that subjects are using mental imagery to make their same/different judgments?

2. Think of 3 real-life examples in which you have used 3-D rotation to solve a problem, or simply review a visual memory.

Mental Scanning

> **How to:** Focus on the center of the screen. A pattern of 4 dots
> will appear for several seconds, followed by an arrow. Press the
> **m**-key if the arrow points to where a dot had been, and press the
> **c**-key if the arrow does not point to one of the previous dots. Be
> sure to keep your right index finger on the **m**-key and your left
> index finger on the **c**-key, and respond as quickly but as accurately
> as possible. You will be given feedback about whether you are
> correct or not, and the next trial will begin in a few seconds.
> There will be 3 practice trials, then 32 real trials.

Your friend Howard asks, "Is it longer from Boston to Atlanta, Georgia, or
to Raleigh, North Carolina?" After wondering why Howard didn't take more
geography classes, you conjure up a mental map, and conclude that Atlanta
is farther from Boston.

How did you answer Howard's question? It seems as if you constructed
a mental map, then scanned down from Boston to North Carolina, then on
to Atlanta, concluding that Atlanta is farther south. This is known as **mental
scanning** (you may also have used scanning to answer the question about
the windows in your house in the Mental Rotation, 3-D ZAP experiment).

This ZAP experiment asks you to temporarily memorize a 4-dot pattern
in each trial. An arrow then points to where one of the dots has been (or has
not). Sometimes in the positive trials, the dot is farther away from one of the
dots, requiring you to mentally scan to where a dot has been. Other research
on mental scanning has used more realistic stimuli, such as pictures of objects
and maps.

Kosslyn, Ball, and Reiser (1978) asked experiment participants to study
a fictional map of an island containing landmarks such as a tree, a pond, a
wishing well, marshy grasses. Subjects had to memorize the map. They then

heard one landmark ("pond") and had to press a button when they mentally scanned to a second landmark ("wishing well"). People's scanning times were linearly related to the actual distance between landmarks; the longer the distance, the longer the response times.

Finke (1989) claimed that this supports his principle of **spatial equivalence** for visual images. In other words, just as it would take you longer to visually scan from the nose of a dog to its tail than from its nose to the collar around its neck, it takes longer in visual imagery to scan longer distances. Thus, a visual image is similar to a picture in that distance between points must be represented. Relative distance and size—spatial properties— are a part of images in the same way as they are of actual pictures.

Kerr (1983) found that even the mental images of blind people had spatial properties. Congenitally blind subjects learned a map with landmarks (distinctive shapes) tactually. They were then asked to "scan" from one landmark to another. As with Kosslyn's experiment, scanning times were related to the actual distance between the landmarks.

Name: _____

Class: _____

Professor: _____

Date: _____

ZAPS: MENTAL SCANNING

Questions

1. Do you think that the blind subjects in Kerr's experiment had a "visual" image in the same way that sighted subjects do? Is there an alternate type of representation that could retain spatial information?

2. When Kosslyn designed his fictional map of the island, he made sure only to ask subjects to scan from one landmark to another when there were no intervening landmarks. Why did he do this? Would intervening items have had any impact on reaction times during the scanning experiment? Why (or why not)?

ZAPS | Misconceptions

How to: Your task in this ZAP is to draw the path of a moving object. Click on one of 3 pictures, then press the **Start** button. Read the instructions before each task very thoroughly. Once each task starts, your computer mouse can be used as a pencil to draw the pathway of the moving object in that task. Press the **Check** button to see if you are correct on each task. There are 10 tasks. Your overall responses to each problem will appear at the end.

While watching a video of Road Runner cartoons, you see Wile E. Coyote run off a cliff, hang suspended in midair, and then fall. The anvil that he has been carrying remains in midair long enough to drop on Wile E. Coyote's head after he hits the ground. Why is this funny? How do you know that the cartoonists have taken liberty with essential laws of physics?

A second scenario: While traveling to grandma's house in a car with the family, your pesky little brother grabs your psychology textbook. He then opens his window and holds the book out the window to taunt you. Oops! When you try to grab him to retrieve your book, little brother drops it onto the highway. If your car was traveling 60 mph at the time, what was the trajectory that your book took as it fell to the ground?

This ZAP asks you to predict the trajectory of a number of items—balls, a suitcase, a truck—in a variety of scenarios. Research in **naïve physics** explores how people reason about events in the physical world without necessarily having any formal training in physics. Kaiser, Jonides, and Alexander (1986) showed subjects a series of curved objects—a coiled hose, a shotgun with a spiral in its barrel. The researchers asked what the trajectory of water would be if it came out of the coiled hose, or how a bullet would fly out of the malformed shotgun. Although subjects were accurate in answering questions about problems that were familiar to them (e.g., we've all washed the car with a hose that was twisted or coiled), they were less accurate when asked to reason about the trajectories of objects out of less familiar items. Furthermore, Kaiser and colleagues found minimal differences between those with physics background and those without!

When subjects were asked to provide rationales for their answers, one of the most common assumptions was that an object's path is influenced by its speed, or that its pathway could still be influenced by the shape of the object out of which it had passed.

What allows us to laugh at the violations of physics principles in Warner Brothers cartoons but give incorrect answers in naïve physics experiments? People often appear to reason about physics principles based on their **mental models**. When asked to predict the trajectory of an object out of a curved tube, or the direction that gears will turn, they mentally construct an image-like representation. This representation can be based on abstract (but potentially incorrect) rules about how the world works, or by analogy to physical phenomena in the world.

Renee Baillargeon constructed some interesting experiments to show that even infants develop notions of naïve physics. She compared children's looking times for "possible" events to "impossible" events. For example, an infant is seated in front of a small stage on which a small box is stacked on top of a larger box. A gloved hand reaches out and pushes the small box to the end of the large box, making sure that the small box still rests entirely on the large one. This is the "possible" event. In another trial, the gloved hand pushes the small box entirely off the large box, but it doesn't fall! This is the impossible event. Baillargeon found that even three-month-old infants looked longer at the impossible event, because they were surprised that the small box did not fall once it lost contact with the large box.

In another condition, the gloved hand left only 15% of the small box resting on the large box (yet the small box did not fall as it should have). Six-and-a-half-month-old infants showed surprise and longer looking times in this impossible condition. In 3.5 months, infants become more sophisticated in their ability to reason about naïve physics problems.

For those who got some answers wrong in the Misconceptions ZAP experiment, you will be soothed to know that the principles being tested in the ZAP are more complex and less obvious than the principles on which the infants were tested in Baillargeon's experiments (it's not that you have not become less smart about physics since you were a baby!).

ZAPS: MISCONCEPTIONS

Questions

1. Would you predict a different trajectory for your psychology book (dropped out the window by little brother) if your car had been traveling 25 mph (rather than the 60 mph mentioned in the example)? Why or why not? Which of the ZAP problems does the dropped psychology book most resemble?

2. Which set of the ZAP problems did you do best with? Worst? If there was a difference, why do you think you were more accurate at applying physics principles to some problems than others? How much physics do you think a person would need to solve all the problems correctly?

3. Spend a Saturday morning watching cartoons (preferably some of the classic Warner Brothers cartoons). Jot down as many examples as you can of traditional physics being violated.

ZAPS | Missionaries and Cannibals

> **How to:** You will see a picture of 2 river "banks" (the rectangles in the water). On the left bank are 3 missionaries and 3 cannibals, with a boat that can hold 2 people. Your task is to drag 1 or 2 people into the boat on each turn, and click the **Start** button to transport it across the river to the other side. In as few moves as possible, get all 6 people safely across. However, 1 person always has to bring back the boat, and cannibals can never outnumber missionaries on any riverbank (or they will eat the missionaries). You will be told if you make a move that is not legal.

Imagine any given week during the semester: You have to turn in the draft of an English paper, take an exam in psychology, send a birthday present to your mother, buy shampoo and toothpaste, and register for next semester's classes. Some of these tasks require several steps—you may have to buy a birthday card and gift for your mother, get wrapping paper and tape, wrap the gift, sign the card, and then take the whole package to the post office. In studying for your psychology exam, you may read and highlight the chapters, make flashcards of relevant terminology, and reread class notes.

Many problems that we encounter—solving algebra homework, repairing a bicycle, figuring out how to accomplish 10 errands in a given day—can be solved in a step-by-step fashion. Missionaries and Cannibals is one such problem: it requires you to get 3 missionaries and 3 cannibals across a river, using a 2-person boat, without allowing any of the cannibals to eat the missionaries.

Researchers have programmed computers to play Missionaries and Cannibals, and other well-defined problems (such as chess), where the end goal, and the steps to accomplish it, are clear and straightforward. When researchers program a computer to play chess (such as "Deep Blue," which has beat chess master Gary Kasparov once) or Missionaries and Cannibals, they also do so in a step-by-step fashion. The computer must be "told" the **initial state** (3 missionaries and 3 cannibals on one side of the river), the **goal state** (get all 3 missionaries and 3 cannibals to the other side of the river safely), and the legal moves to do so (called the **operators**). It also must be informed of any **constraints**—such as the fact that cannibals can never outnumber missionaries on one side (or they'll eat the missionaries), and that only 2 people can fit in the boat.

Operators come in 2 forms: **algorithms** *guarantee* a solution—if the computer were able to calculate *all* possible combinations of moves to see which one resulted in a solution fastest, it would be using algorithms. Although a powerful computer could do this quickly, it would not be a time-efficient strategy for humans. **Heuristics**, on the other hand, are strategies that make a solution more likely, but do not guarantee a solution. For example, you may have had a subgoal to get all the missionaries across first, so that they would form a critical mass on the goal state side of the river, and you wouldn't need to worry about them being eaten as you continued to transport cannibals across to the goal side.

A good way to illustrate the difference between algorithms and heuristics is with the use of anagrams (or scrambled words). Try to unscramble these 2 words:

DFELID
OROETCS

Did you start listing every possible combination of letters for each anagram? Probably not—this would have constituted use of an algorithm. If you had listed every possible combination for the scrambled words, *at least one* of the combinations would have been a correct answer, and thus you'd have been guaranteed a solution. More likely, you used your knowledge of how English words are composed to start with common combinations of letters—in the first anagram, you may have known that double letters (the *d*s) were likely to appear together, and that *l* and *e* often occur together at the end of words. Then, *voila*, the answer fell into place (answer at end of the page). Likewise, for the second anagram, you may have put the two *o*s together, and the *er* at the end of a word before realizing the answer. Knowing frequent combinations of letters in English increased your likelihood of solving each anagram (but didn't guarantee it). However, it appears that heuristics may be more common strategies for humans to use than are algorithms.

One heuristic you may have used in the Missionaries and Cannibals problem is **difference reduction**—with each step, you tried to reduce the difference between the initial and the goal state. With each trip across the river, the strategy was to leave 1 more person on the goal side than there had been on the prior move. However, you were forced to adjust this heuristic

in the step where 2 people had to transport the boat back to the initial side (thereby *not* increasing the number of people on the goal side during that trip). Instead, the more flexible **means-end analysis heuristic** proved more useful and enabled you to solve the problem. You knew the desired *end* result (all 3 missionaries and 3 cannibals safely across the river), and the *means* available to you (2-person boat, etc.), and thus took whatever steps necessary to ultimately solve the problem, even if it meant undoing some of your progress in one step. You might also have used the **working backward** heuristic to solve the Missionaries and Cannibals problem—since the goal state was to have all 3 missionaries and all 3 cannibals on the other side of the river without cannibals eating any missionaries, you may have thought that the last move would be to move 2 cannibals over (with one cannibal and three missionaries already safely on the goal bank). Then, the second to last move was for 1 cannibal to take the boat back for the last remaining cannibal on the initial bank. And the third to last move would be . . . And so on, until you worked backward from the goal to the initial state (instead of initial to goal).

Another useful heuristic that we use on a regular basis is **analogical transfer**—the use of a familiar problem to solve a new problem. You use analogies even without realizing it: if your friend lets you drive her car, you automatically get into the car and insert the key without bothering to search around for the ignition. How? You automatically (and unconsciously) infer that your friend's car is similar to your own car, and thus try to insert the key in the ignition in the same place.

After completing the Missionaries and Cannibals experiment, try solving this problem on paper:

> **HOBBITS AND ORCS:** Three hobbits and 3 orcs arrive at a riverbank to find a boat holding 2 creatures. Both sets of creatures want to cross to the other side. However, the orcs are very vicious and will attack the peaceful hobbits if they ever outnumber them on a river bank. How many steps will it take to get the 3 hobbits and 3 orcs across the river safely, without the orcs ever attacking the hobbits?

Don't you think it will be much easier to solve the Hobbits and Orcs problem now that you know the solution to the Missionaries and Cannibals problem? That is an example of analogical transfer.

Answers to Anagrams: FIDDLE and SCOOTER

ZAPS: MISSIONARIES AND CANNIBALS

Questions

1. Could you program a computer to play checkers? Candyland?
   Monopoly? Pictionary? Why or why not? Choose one of these
   games and explain what rules you might institute to enable a
   computer to play (and perhaps win) that game.

2. What heuristics or strategies do you use when you play a game like
   Monopoly? Do you tend to amass as much cash as possible before
   buying properties, or do you concentrate on building your real estate?
   Do you put houses on all your properties, or put hotels on a few
   properties to maximize your rent from those?

3. Can you think of a real-life situation in which you were forced to
   "undo" some of your progress to solve a problem (like in Missionaries
   and Cannibals)? How long did it take you to realize this was the best
   move (in real life)? What strategies did you attempt first?

| Moral Development

> **How to:** Select one of the 3 moral dilemmas (Heinz, Bob and Karl, Doctor and Ill Woman), read that story, and answer **yes** or **no** to the question at the end. You will then be shown 6 arguments in favor of your answer. Rank them from 1 to 6, in order of moral complexity (based on Kohlberg's theory of moral development). When you click on a sentence you can move it up or down to change its rank. You can also use the cursor keys to move a sentence around. When you think the sequence of arguments is in the correct order, press **Check**. If there are mistakes in sequence, you will be told so. You can repeat putting the sentences in the correct sequence. After 3 tries, you can also see the correct sequence by pressing the **Reveal** button.
>
> If you have difficulty, read the Theory section of this ZAP first, then attempt the Experience section.

A little boy named John is called to dinner. Behind the door to the dining room is a chair with 15 cups on it. John does not know this, so when he opens the door, he breaks all 15 cups! Another little boy named Henry tried to get some jam out of a cupboard when his mother was out. He climbed onto the cupboard, knocked over a cup and broke it! Which little boy is naughtier?

Piaget (1932, 1965) posed such stories to children, and found that children under age 6 typically said that John was the naughtier boy, because he had broken 15 cups. Older children claimed that Henry was naughtier because he was intentionally trying to sneak jam when he broke the cup, whereas John broke the 15 cups by accident. The children's responses led Piaget to conclude that there are 2 stages of moral reasoning—an early stage that only takes into account the consequences of an action (so breaking 15 cups is worse than breaking 1), and a later stage that emphasizes intention (Henry is deliberately doing something naughty).

Lawrence Kohlberg later expanded Piaget's notions on moral development, to include 6 overall stages within 3 levels:

Preconventional Level

Stage 1: Avoiding punishment is the main reason for good behavior.

Stage 2: Self-interest and meeting one's personal needs guides moral decision making.

Conventional Level

Stage 3: The approval of one's family and friends is the main motivation for moral behavior.

Stage 4: A law and order rationale is prevalent; people must obey rules for society to work effectively.

Postconventional Level

Stage 5: Rules are based on a social contract, and can be altered to achieve the evolving goals of society.

Stage 6: Abstract universal principles of right and wrong (e.g., the sanctity of human life) provide the basis for moral decision making.

Kohlberg's theory is designed to explain moral judgments, not whether people are able to translate their beliefs into moral actions. Research has shown that there is a developmental trend from Stage 1 and 2 moral reasoning to Stage 3 and then Stage 4. However, Kohlberg warned, very few people achieve postconventional reasoning.

Kohlberg's theory of moral development has been criticized as chauvinistic on several levels. First, it is claimed that his theory is culturally biased. Very few non-Westerners achieve postconventional levels of reasoning, and many non-Western societies would find Stage 5 and 6 reasoning baffling. The emphasis on abstract principles as the basis for moral judgments appears to be uniquely revered in the United States and Europe. Critics have questioned whether Kohlberg really wanted to claim that the rest of the world is immature relative to the reasoning of Westerners. Second, Carol Gilligan and others have claimed that Kohlberg's theory is sexist. It was formulated on the basis of interviews with only males. Furthermore, she found that females tend to reason based on caregiving and maintaining social relationships (Stage 3) rather than abstract notions of justice (embodied in Stages 4, 5, and 6). Given females' typical caregiver roles, Gilligan says that their values are *different* than those of males, not more immature.

ZAPS: MORAL DEVELOPMENT

Questions

1. Why does the intention to do wrong play such an important part in our judgments of morality? Since research shows that even young children can understand other people's intentions, why do you think they don't use intention in moral judgments to the same extent as older children or adults?

2. If asked, what would have been your justification for each of your answers to the Heinz Dilemma, Bob and Karl, and Doctor and Ill Woman moral scenarios? What level of morality would these responses have placed you in Kohlberg's stages? Would you have been placed in the same stage of moral reasoning on all 3 dilemmas?

3. What factors do you think most influence our development of morality? Parents? Extended family? Friends? Media? Religion? The culture overall? Which factors have been most influential in your development of morality? Have these factors changed since you were young?

ZAPS | Obsessive-Compulsive Disorder

> **How to:** The practice phase of this experiment allows you to turn on and off 6 gas rings on a stove, and then 6 light bulbs. As you practice these tasks, remember that a gas ring or light bulb can be on without appearing to be lit. The actual experiment will give you a series of 8 activities involving the gas rings and light bulbs. Perform all the tasks and answer the questionnaire at the end. Next, you will be asked to solve a few puzzles. Solve all the puzzles to the best of your ability; there is a time limit for this section. Part II of the real experiment will then begin. Perform all the gas ring/light bulb tasks and answer the questionnaire. Your data will appear at the end.

Have you ever fallen into bed, only to wonder if you locked the front door? Or worried all day that you forgot to turn off the coffee pot when you left that morning and may return to a home charred by a coffee-pot fire? We all worry about things sporadically. For people with obsessive-compulsive disorder, however, such worrisome thoughts occur repeatedly and often disrupt their daily lives. **Obsessions** are frequent, disturbing thoughts, whereas **compulsions** are the repetitive behaviors that often accompany obsessions. For example, alarming thoughts about germs (obsessions) may lead to constant hand washing and house cleaning (compulsions), sometimes even resulting in raw hands, or hours each day spent cleaning the same parts of the house. **Obsessive-compulsive disorder** (OCD) may interfere with a person's job, social and family life, and ability to live a normal life.

People with OCD report that fears and thoughts intrude, and that they are unable to reason themselves out of such fears. For example, one fear reported by patients is that they forgot to turn off the gas stove before going to bed. Checking the stove, though, is insufficient to allay their fears. An

OCD patient may check 5 or 10 or even 20 times to make sure that they have turned off the gas stove. This is not because of a memory deficit (they remember that they have already checked the stove), but rather a drive to alleviate the anxiety caused by the obsessions. The time dedicated to compulsions may eat up much of a day for OCD patients.

One hypothesis for how compulsions start and continue is through operant conditioning. Because checking the gas stove alleviates some (but not all) anxiety, it serves as **reinforcement**. The behavior gets repeated again, and again, because even a mild reduction in anxiety feels better. There is also evidence that the cause of OCD may be genetic in some cases. Some symptoms of the disorder (as well as the full-blown disorder) may run in families. Furthermore, abnormalities in brain structure and brain-wave patterns have been found in patients with obsessive-compulsive disorder. Patients with OCD have been found to show overactivity in the frontal lobes, those parts of the brain related to planning.

OCD is most common in teenagers and young adults, and most people's symptoms improve as they get older. One famous exception was Howard Hughes, the billionaire businessman and movie producer. His OCD became worse over time, until he died a recluse who refused to eat much, had let his finger- and toenails grow to a grotesque length, and spent most of his time in a darkened room trying to avoid germs. He was so wealthy that he could afford to have his employees carry out compulsive rituals (such as using seven or eight tissues to open a bathroom door to prevent spreading germs).

Some sufferers report relief after taking antidepressant drugs, or a combination of drugs and psychotherapy.

ZAPS: OBSESSIVE-COMPULSIVE DISORDER

Questions

1. Do you tend to worry about the same things all the time (e.g., having locked the door), or do your worries differ through time? Do you have any rituals or habits that are designed to prevent you from worrying, or to remind you to do important things? How might these rituals be similar to the ones OCD patients exhibit? How are they different?

2. Why do you think that people with OCD can't use their intellect to help them get over their obsessions and compulsions? What types of therapy do you think would be most effective in changing the thoughts and habits of OCD patients, and why?

3. How are obsessions related to phobias? How are they different?

| Operation Span

> **HOW TO:** In each trial, you will see a math problem and be asked to determine whether the equation is correct or not. Next, a word will appear, then another math problem, another word, and so on. Your task is to concentrate on the math problems to see if the equation is correct, and to remember the words in order per trial. After anywhere from 2 to 7 math problem/word pairings are presented per trial, you will see a list of words. Click on them in the order in which they appeared.

Normally, we divide memory into short-term memory and long-term memory. This is consistent with historical accounts of memory dating back to the time of Aristotle, up to the 1950s Multistore Memory model of Shiffrin and Atkinson. In the Multistore Model, however, STM is considered to be a temporary **store** for information before it's either lost or makes its way into long-term store. Alan Baddeley thought it better to replace the concept of STM with **working memory**—a place where information can be both stored *and* processed. For example, you can keep in mind a set of groceries that you need to buy while also calculating the cost of those groceries. The traditional notion of STM and Baddeley's concept of working memory both posit that we can only hold a limited amount of information.

This ZAP experiment tests your operation span—the number of items that you can hold in working memory while still processing information. The operation scan score is the total number of items (out of 40) that you could remember in order across the test trials. The experiment requires you both to hold information in memory (the words presented) and process information at the same time (calculate whether the math problems are correct or not).

and which strategy or pathway is used to remember information.

In a set of interesting experiments, Baddeley, Thomson, and Buchanan (1975) found that counting from one to eight repeatedly interfered with remembering information in the phonological loop. Quinn and McConnell (1996) found that subjects using visual mnemonics to remember a list of words had their memory interfered with a visual noise task. These experiments support the notion of a separate phonological loop and visual-spatial sketchpad to rehearse information verbally or visually, respectively. These findings also support Baddeley's contention that *visual* information will most disrupt material that you are trying to remember in the visual-spatial sketchpad, and *verbal* information will most interfere with material being processed in the phonological loop.

ZAPS: OPERATION SPAN

Questions

1. In the ZAP experiment, would you have used the phonological loop or visual-spatial sketchpad to try to remember the words sandwiched in between the math problems? Which rehearsal loop would mentally calculating the math problems be most likely to interrupt?

2. When might you be most likely to use the visual-spatial sketchpad to remember information? What types of mathematics-related problems might be most likely to interfere with the memory for visual information?

ZAPS | Ponzo Illusion

HOW TO: In the Experience phase of this ZAP, several oblique lines (vertical lines slanted inward) and two horizontal lines will appear. Your job is to make the two horizontal lines the exact same length. To do so, use the "shorter" and "longer" icons at the bottom of the figure to shorten or lengthen the bottom horizontal line. Click on "check" to see if you have made the lines equal or not.

You may also use the "more" and "less" icons to increase or decrease the number of oblique lines. The "again" icon will provide you with a new trial.

In the Experiment phase, you will receive 10 trials. On each trial, shorten or lengthen the bottom horizontal line to make the two horizontal lines equal. Click "check" when you think you have succeeded. Data will be presented at the end of the 10 trials to show whether you've successfully made the 2 lines equal or not.

Remember junior high art class, when your art teacher taught you about creating the sense of depth or perspective in your drawings? And he had you draw a set of railroad tracks converging into the distance—wide at the "close" end and narrow at the "far-away" end? This is a standard artist's technique, known as **linear perspective** (or **linear convergence**) that is used to illustrate depth on a 2-dimensional piece of canvas.

The linear perspective's ability to trick the eyes into perceiving relative distance is at the heart of the Ponzo illusion.

There are 2 major ways that our eyes perceive depth or 3-dimensions:

a. **Binocular disparity** (or stereopsis): Two different images fall on the retina of each eye. How to test this? With both eyes open, hold one index finger up and align it with some edge in the room (a corner, edge of the blackboard). Close first one eye, then the other. Did your finger appear to jump or misalign when either the left or the right eye was closed? The 2 different retinal images represent the same object (your finger), but from a slightly different perspective (given that our eyes are a couple of inches apart). When these 2 different images are combined in the brain, you perceive one 3-dimensional representation.

The Ponzo illusion (and many other illusions) are based on:

b. **Monocular depth cues**, which are similar to the ones artists use to depict depth or distance, and only require the use of one eye. For example, *texture gradient* gives us cues as to the relative depth of objects—you can see the fine detail in the sweater of the person sitting next to you, but not of the sweater on the person all the way across a large lecture hall. The person sitting next to you also impinges on more of your retina than the person sitting across the lecture hall (*relative size*, another monocular cue).

However, your perceptual system also corrects for relative size—it allows you to perceive the person sitting next to you as closer, but you don't believe that he is twice as large as the person sitting across the lecture hall (even if the retinal image is twice the retinal image of the farther person). This is called **size constancy**. If the classmate sitting next to you gets up and walks to the other side of the room, you don't perceive her as shrinking, only as getting farther away.

The Ponzo illusion, then, is based both on the monocular depth cue of linear perspective and on size constancy. Because our visual system interprets the oblique, vertical lines as converging into the distance, it judges the top horizontal line to be farther away. Then, because the top and bottom horizontal lines are actually the same size (as they fall on the retina), the one that is "farther away" (the top) *must* be longer (says our visual system).

Many other visual illusions, such as the **Müller-Lyer illusion** and the **moon illusion**, are based on some combination of the use of monocular distance cues and size constancy. Our perceptions and visual judgments are based not only on what we see but also on our brain's calculation of what we see *within a given context.*

ZAPS: PONZO ILLUSION

Questions

1. Look out the window, or around your house or apartment, and find 4 or 5 depth or distance cues.

2. Are distance cues innate or learned? Do you think tribal peoples who grow up in more natural surroundings (without skyscrapers, bridges, etc.) will be prone to visual illusions in the same way that we are?

3. In addition to size constancy, we are also subject to shape constancy—a coffee cup is still judged as round even when we look at its aperture from an angle (so that an elliptical shape of the cup opening falls on our retina). Can you find 3 other examples of shape constancy around you?

ZAPS | Prisoner's Dilemma

HOW TO: The Discovery section of this ZAP allows you to experiment with different strategies in the prisoner's dilemma (detailed in the Introduction). Your task is to earn points. Select a strategy for each player, and then press the **Start** button. The game will then run by itself through 25 turns on the part of each player. Scores for each player will be depicted in a graph. At the end of game 1, you may either maintain each player's strategy, or alter the strategy of one (or both). It is worth altering the strategies of one or both players in multiple games to see the relative worth of each strategy combination. You may also select one of three matrices: **Classic**, **Lift** (extra points are given when the two players differ in strategy), and **Chicken** (which poses heavy penalties when both players defect).

In the Experience section, you will play an iterated prisoner's dilemma against the computer. First select a strategy for the computer to use (the option of **Surprise** has now been added as a strategy). On each turn, you will then choose **Cooperate** or **Defect**, and the computer will then respond. You and the computer each take 10 turns. Your goal is to earn as many points as possible; the results of each turn will be shown in a graph. After the 10 turns are up, overall scores will be shown, as well as the strategy that the computer used. Multiple games may be played by pressing **Again**.

Jack and Jill have a baby, Mary, Mary Quite Contrary. They must decide whether to get Mary, Mary Quite Contrary immunized against polio, diphtheria, whooping cough, chicken pox, and hepatitis. If they don't get their baby immunized, she might contract some of these serious diseases, and pass on the illnesses to other children. However, if a significant number of other people immunize their children, then Mary, Mary Quite Contrary might not contract those diseases because many will have been wiped out in the general population. This is a social dilemma, similar to that posed in the prisoner's dilemma, because it pits self-interest against the interests (and the responses) of someone else (in this case, the general population).

As long as everyone else in the population is immunized, Jack and Jill don't really need to immunize their daughter, as she is unlikely to catch diseases from immunized people. Thus, they can save the $250 they would have spent on immunization shots toward a family vacation. However, what if other people in the population reason the same way? Then, there will be children from whom Mary, Mary Quite Contrary can catch diseases. In this case, it is worth the money for Jack and Jill to immunize their daughter to avoid her succumbing to serious diseases. Although this decision might seem like a no-brainer to us—since the potential risks of not immunizing are serious illness and death, Jack and Jill should just pay $250 to keep their daughter safe. However, there are contemporary parents who do not immunize their children because they count on everyone else to do it (imagine that $250 means the difference between being able to pay rent or being evicted).

In the prisoner's dilemma, two guilty burglars have to decide whether to confess to the crime, not knowing what their partner has done. The dilemma is that if neither of them confesses, they will receive a minimal jail term. If both confess, they'll both receive a moderate sentence, because at least they cooperated with the police. However, if only *one* confesses (but not the other), whichever one confesses will receive a much lighter sentence. Thus, the outcome of one burglar's decision depends on the other burglar's decision (much like in the immunization example).

The prisoner's dilemma and other social dilemmas have been useful research tools in psychology, decision making, economics, politics, and other fields. Analysis of when people or nations are most likely to cooperate with each other has led to formulas within **game theory**, the branch of mathematics concerned with developing formal predictions for when it is most useful for people to cooperate or not within a given situation. If you have seen the movie *A Beautiful Mind*, you may remember the scene in the bar when the John Nash character (played by Russell Crowe) argues that the most adaptive strategy for getting dates is not for he and his friends to compete for the attentions of the most beautiful woman, but rather to ignore the most beautiful woman and all approach that woman's friends. If they compete for the beautiful woman, only one will win (maybe), whereas the other strategy assures more of them will have dates for the evening. Despite its name, game theory often has important consequences.

Of course, some of these same social dilemmas arise within animal groups. Think of two dogs that meet each other in the park and must decide whether to attack each other or to be submissive by showing their underbelly (and thus avoiding a fight). If both are submissive, they will both avoid injuries and perhaps have fun chasing each other. If both attack, they will both sustain pain and injuries, but neither will be defenseless. However, if only one dog attacks and the other is submissive, then the submissive one will receive the most serious injuries. As with the prisoner's dilemma, the best strategy is dependent on what the other dog does. Scientists now routinely use game theory to explain biological phenomena and evolutionarily based behaviors.

ZAPS: PRISONER'S DILEMMA

Questions

1. Research has shown that negative campaigning by candidates is often effective; criticizing an opponent publicly leads people to think less highly of that opponent. How does the prisoner's dilemma relate to negative campaign ads? What should be the most effective strategy of a candidate who has been the victim of negative campaigning—should he then fire negative ads at the other candidate or not?

2. Historical situations in which game theory has been relevant involve Cold War episodes such as the Bay of Pigs, and peace treaties between Israelis and Palestinians. Explain how each of these political conflicts relates to the prisoner's dilemma?

3. What other real-life examples of the prisoner's dilemma can you recall?

| Recalling Information

HOW TO: You will be shown a list of 20 words, one at a time. Try to memorize them as best you can. Next, you will be asked to recall the words (be sure to spell them correctly when you type). In a second phase, you will be given hints to help you recall words that you did not originally recall.

Your professor announces a pop quiz that day on all the psychology terminology you've learned the past two weeks. She says it will be a fill-in-the-blank quiz: You will be provided with a definition and have to retrieve the proper term that fits the definition. The class gives a collective "Ughhh!" But then the professor says, "But since attendance has been good, I've also provided you with the first letter of each psychology term." The class now gives a collective "Yeah!" because everyone knows that having some hint is better than no hint when you're trying to retrieve information from memory.

This ZAP illustrates the difference in difficulty between retrieving information spontaneously from memory (**free recall**) versus retrieving information with a hint (**cued recall**). We have already seen that it is important to *encode* information, and *store* it appropriately. But unless we can show evidence of being able to *retrieve* information, someone might doubt that we had ever learned it to begin with. Imagine that you're trying to think of the name of the physicist who helped to discover the atomic bomb. You can't remember his name until someone says, "It starts with an O," and you then retrieve "Oppenheimer."

Sometimes subjects can make use of their own retrieval cues to facilitate memory. In a classic historical experiment, Bousfield presented people with a list of 60 words taken from 4 categories (e.g., fruits). Even though the words were presented in random order, subjects tended to recall the words in category clusters. Thus, even if "apple" and "banana" were separated by

5 words, recalling "apple" acts as a retrieval cue for "banana" and all other fruit words.

Another way of retrieving information that's been stored in memory is through a **recognition test** (which some of the other ZAP memory experiments utilize). Who wouldn't prefer a multiple-choice test to a fill-in-the-blank exam? At least on the multiple-choice exam, the correct answer is provided along with a few **foils** (wrong answers). You don't need to spontaneously retrieve the answer, only to pick out the correct answer out of 4 (or 2 or 3, or 5) options. Multiple-choice tests illustrate what is known as a forced choice recognition task—you are forced to choose which out of several options is the correct answer, or (on a memory test) the word you heard during the learning phase of an experiment.

Shepard (1967) conducted a classic experiment on recognition memory for both words and pictures. He found that even 3 days after viewing 612 pictures, subjects were 92% accurate at choosing which of two pictures they had seen in a forced choice recognition task. Such high performance is much better than usually discovered for verbal material. This became known as the **picture superiority effect**, which is now well documented in cognitive psychology. Shepard also found evidence for a **word frequency effect** in memory: high-frequency words (such as *office, woman*) are better recalled than rare, low-frequency words (such as *synergy, ferule*). However, in a forced choice recognition task, Shepard found that low-frequency words were better remembered (around 92% versus average of 84% for high-frequency words). Why? If an uncommon word is right in front of you, as in a recognition task, it is easy to pick out because it is so distinctive. This interaction between word frequency and type of retrieval test is known as the word frequency effect.

Name: _____

Class: _____

Professor: _____

Date: _____

ZAPS: RECALLING INFORMATION

Questions

1. Think of 2 or 3 occasions in which you could not retrieve the name of a movie star, or a science term, but were aided by a retrieval cue.

2. How does this ZAP relate to the one on encoding specificity? What serves as the retrieval cue in state-dependent memory, or context effects in memory?

ZAPS | Recognizing Emotions

HOW TO: After pressing **Start**, you will be presented with a face. Identify which emotion the person is expressing from the array of 7 emotional states and click on the emotion. Twenty-eight faces will appear and feedback about your responses will be provided at the end.

You agree to meet your friend at the cafeteria for lunch at noon. At 12:15, you look down at your watch and realize that you're late. Arriving at the cafeteria, your friend's furrowed eyebrows and frowning mouth send the message that your friend is angry. You start your apology before you even get to the table. Furthermore, everyone else in the cafeteria can tell your friend is angry. How do we do this?

Charles Darwin, in his book, *The Expression of Emotions in Man and Animals,* claimed that the expression of emotional states (and the ability to recognize those emotional states) is hard-wired into us because it provides evolutionary advantages. Even if you are a dog lover, you are unlikely to try and pet a snarling dog with its teeth showing. Why? The dog's emotional expression is threatening and indicative of its desire to bite should you get too close. On the other hand, a panting dog with a frantically wagging tail appears friendly and open to being petted. From a human standpoint, almost all children have experienced "the look" from mom or dad while misbehaving in public—the one that says you are in big trouble once you get back home. How do all parents acquire the same "look," and how do all children recognize it? Darwin would argue that being able to send signals of warning (like parents) and to identify warning signals in others (as the children do) are adaptive, and thus are innate.

Paul Ekman has studied how people from different cultures express (and recognize) emotions. He asked American actors to convey a variety of emotions, such as sadness, fear, joy, and anger. When these photos were shown to Swedish, Japanese, and Kenyan subjects, and even New Guinea tribesman, they were able to identify the emotions depicted by the American actors. This was true in reverse as well; American students could identify the emotions expressed by the New Guinea tribesmen. In other words, the expression and recognition of many emotions is *universal* across cultures.

Researchers have concluded that there are at least five **basic emotions**: anger, fear, disgust, sadness, and joy/happiness. Ekman (1984) also included surprise and contempt; Carroll Izard included surprise and infant. One of Izard's key interests was in the development of emotions in infants. He found that emotional expressions are indeed universal in infants and young children, and are universally interpreted by parents and caregivers. Izard also objectively catalogued the facial features that make up each type of expression, and showed that infants' facial expressions are accompanied by underlying physiological and emotional states.

The universality of emotional expression and emotional development are both used as evidence that emotional display is innate. One further piece of evidence is that even people who are blind from birth (and thus have never seen other people's emotional expressions) still smile, frown, laugh, and cry at stimuli that typically cause sighted people to smile, frown, laugh, or cry. However, the appropriateness of emotional displays within a given context clearly has a learned component. A 3-year-old who opens a birthday gift containing an unwanted pair of hand-knit socks from Grandma might say, "I don't like these." However, a 7-year-old knows that she should express pleasure in front of Grandma (even while vowing inwardly never to be seen dead in the socks). The 7-year-old has learned the appropriate **display rules** for that situation. More complex emotions also have a learned component. For example, guilt or shame would be difficult to feel (or express) without having learned moral or societal rules—both guilt and shame are feelings of sadness or anxiety toward oneself about having violated certain moral codes.

ZAPS: RECOGNIZING EMOTIONS

Questions

1. Did you wrongly identify any of the emotions in the ZAP demonstration? Which expressions could most easily be confused with each other?

2. Lists of the "basic emotions" range from 5 to 10. Are there any other emotions you would want to include (or exclude) in a list of basic emotions beyond the seven tested by this ZAP exercise? Why? Can you think of any evidence why your inclusions are basic emotions?

3. Do you think there's a difference between faking an emotional expression versus expressing a real emotional state? Which should be easier to recognize and why? How do the best actors appear so convincing when conveying emotions? What techniques would you use to convey emotion if you were to act in a play or movie?

How to: This ZAP is an example of a selection test that employers might use when deciding who to hire for a given position. This one is geared toward different intellectual skills. There are 20 tasks (5 trials across 4 types of tests). There is no time limit on any trial; take as much time as you need for any given problem. However, if you find yourself taking too long, just guess. Your data will be presented at the end (but there will be no judgments about overall intelligence).

Your dorm is having a dance, and only couples with dates are to be admitted. You're not interested in finding romance, but just want to attend the dance with someone fun and entertaining. You decide to conduct undercover interviews with some of the people on your dorm floor while at dinner, and to observe people as they interact. What types of behaviors will you observe to determine whether someone is fun to be with? What types of questions will you ask? Are these the same behaviors and questions you would be interested in if you were interviewing a tutor to help you with your physics? Probably not—the important traits in a tutor have more to do with someone who understands physics well and can communicate this knowledge clearly, rather than whether the tutor is fun or not.

In your quest for a fun-loving date for the dorm dance (or your search for a physics tutor), you want to look for target behaviors that indicate being fun and entertaining. Whether a person has a blue or a red overcoat, and whether he or she is vegetarian or not, probably won't provide you with any insight about their fun-loving aspects. Laughing at, or telling, funny jokes, and being sociable towards others, however, are valid measures of whether a person might be a fun date. In other words, what you need is validity within your test—it must truly measure whatever traits or skills it claims to, and high measurements on the test should correlate with high marks on the relevant behavior. A test for visual-spatial skills should be able to pick out people who can read maps well. Validity is important for any test—whether it is a personnel selection test, an I.Q. test, a personality test, or a date-finding test. You want to use a measure that is associated with and predicts good performance in a given job or skill. Typing skill is not a valid predictor of being a good artist, nor is avidly reading mystery novels a good predictor of being a good secretary.

Another issue related to constructing tests is **reliability**—the consistency with which a test measures what it purports to. For example, would two researchers looking at the responses of a single person come up with the same score or diagnosis? Would a person taking the test on two separate days have very similar scores on both days? After all, if your test is measuring a trait we think of as being stable—intelligence, personality, creativity— then their scores should not vary greatly from one day to the next (although minor fluctuations in scores are no cause for alarm).

This ZAP acquaints you with tests of numerical skill and reasoning, verbal skills, abstract reasoning, and spatial skill, which might be found on some personnel tests. Sometimes, employers also use personality tests to see if a person has leadership potential or the ability to work well with others. Tests of creativity might be administered to job applicants in fields that need open thinking or artistic sensibilities. The types of tests they use depend on the positions for which they are interviewing.

The history of intelligence testing extends back over 100 years. Alfred Binet was hired by the French government to write a test that could be used to distinguish children who may need extra academic help or special programs. Binet and Theophile Simon wrote questions relating to memory, mathematical skills, reasoning, and so on. Children's scores on the Binet-Simon test were found to correlate with their academic achievement, and thus the test had good predictive validity. This test later became the Stanford-Binet after it was modified and modernized by researchers at Stanford (and is still used today). Most intelligence tests separate skills into verbal and visual, or verbal and math components. The Wechsler tests, among the most widely used intelligence batteries—the WISC for children, and the WAIS for adults— are divided into Verbal (including some math problems) and Performance (geared more toward visual-spatial reasoning) sections.

Some researchers, though, have asserted that intelligence tests, and the definition of intelligence upon which they are based, is too limited. Robert Sternberg has proposed a triarchic theory of intelligence that has analytical, creative, and practical components. Business people with equivalent analytical skills might be hired, but the one with better practical knowledge will make president of the company. Howard Gardner claims that there are multiple intelligences—the traditional linguistic, logical-mathematical, and spatial intelligences, as well as musical, bodily-kinesthetic (such as that shown by gymnasts), and personal intelligences. Gardner based his divisions on studies of which types of skills are controlled by different parts of the brain, and the study of **savants**, who are mentally retarded in most areas but extremely gifted in one of the areas. For instance, the autistic man played by Dustin Hoffman in *Rainman* was based on a real autistic patient who had remarkable mathematical abilities despite an I.Q. within the range of mental retardation.

ZAPS: SELECTION PROCEDURE/I.Q. TEST

Questions

1. If you were an employer, what types of tests would you administer to applicants of an engineering position? A secretarial position? A graphic artist position? What might be the potential downfalls of relying heavily on personnel tests? What additional information might be provided by an interview that is useful in hiring the best person for the job?

2. How do you think that researchers who construct tests make sure that those tests are valid and reliable?

ZAPS | Selective Attention

> **How to:** After clicking **Start**, you will see two columns of words appear for only 15 seconds. Try as best you can to remember the words; you will be asked to recall them directly afterwards. Be sure to spell the words accurately so that they will be counted correctly. A second list of words will then appear, with slightly different directions. Your data (number of correctly remembered words) will appear after each trial.

You attend a campus party. Among the 50 people attending, there are 15 different conversations taking place. If you are asked to try and remember all the topics being talked about for 60 seconds, it will be next to impossible to try to pay attention to all 15 conversations at the same time. However, you should have no trouble paying attention to the conversation of the four people in your group, about your college's basketball team win that night. Focusing on the conversation in which you are immersed, while ignoring the other 14 background conversations, is known as **selective attention**. It involves **filtering** which information you take in, as no one can possibly attend to 15 conversations simultaneously.

Historically, 3 major filter theories of attention have been proposed: Broadbent (1960) claimed that we can only process one message at a time. If listening to two conversations, you will notice the sensory characteristics of both (whether the speaker is male or female, has a high- or a low-pitched voice), but you will only be able to comprehend one of the messages; the other conversation is blocked.

The problem with Broadbent's theory is that it cannot explain the **cocktail party phenomenon**—imagine that you are assiduously paying attention to the conversation about the basketball team, and ignoring the conversation of the three people behind you. However, one of those three people

171

then mentions your best friend's name. At least momentarily, your attention shifts to see if the people behind you are saying something negative about your best friend. If you were fully ignoring the conversation behind you (as Broadbent's model suggests), how did you process your best friend's name to begin with? Anne Treisman proposed that messages we seem to be ignoring may only be **attenuated**, or dampened down. Significant words (like our best friend's name, or our own name, or "fire!") will still get through for recognition, even in a conversation we were ignoring. In the **attenuator model**, one message typically gets through for full processing, but a second one is only partially filtered, permitting recognition of some words.

This brings up the notion of **top-down processing**. Recognizing a message is not only due to the auditory stimulus that we hear, but is also influenced by what we already know. While we might "hear" some of the sounds of an unfamiliar person's name in the ignored conversation behind us, our mind does not recognize the unfamiliar name, nor do we remember it. However, upon processing the sounds of our best friend's name, we are also better to "hear" that name because it is so familiar. In other words, what we know "comes down" to influence perception of the sounds we hear. A visual example of top-down processing can be found in the Word Superiority Effect ZAP.

A third model of selective attention, the **pertinence model** (Norman, 1968; Deutsch & Deutsch, 1963), claims that we process or recognize *both* the basketball conversation in which we are engaged *and* the conversation of the group behind us. However, our cognitive system can only actively remember or respond to one of the messages at a time (whichever one we deem pertinent). By the time you've responded to a question in the basketball conversation, information about the other conversation has faded. Many researchers think, though, that fully processing multiple messages simultaneously would be a waste of our cognitive resources. This third explanation of selective attention does not have as much empirical support as Treisman's attenuator model.

ZAPS: SELECTIVE ATTENTION

Questions

1. Name at least three daily occurrences in which you exhibit selective attention.

2. Do you think it is more difficult to listen to music on two radio stations at the same time, or to listen to music on the radio and look at a book of photographs? Why?

3. Proofreader's error (when you don't notice misspelled words) is another example of top-down processing. Explain how information you already have stored in memory might lead you to permit misspellings in a paper. Why does proofreading accuracy improve if you read the paper *backwards* to check for word misspellings?

Sentence Verification

HOW TO: On each trial, a sentence will appear on the screen. Decide whether the statement is accurate or not. If it is accurate, press the **m**-key; if not accurate, press the **c**-key. Be as fast but as accurate as you can. Keep your right finger on the **m**-key and your left finger on the **c**-key. Feedback will be provided after each response, and the next statement will appear automatically. There are 3 practice trials, then 24 real trials.

Is a bat a bird or a mammal? Does it hang upside down while sleeping? Does it lay eggs? Or bear live young? Does it have skin? This ZAP is not about verifying sentences per se, but about testing what you know about categories and how quickly you can respond to the sentences. Such experiments provide information about how people's semantic category knowledge is structured.

Collins and Quillian (1969) proposed a hypothetical model known as the **hierarchical semantic network model**. It structures category information from the most overarching category (such as ANIMAL) to more specific categories (OSTRICH). The overarching category (ANIMAL) is known as the **superordinate category**; the middle level (BIRDS; FISH) is the **basic level** category; the most specific items (ROBIN; OSTRICH) are **subordinate categories**.

In the hierarchical semantic network, properties about each item are stored at the most general level to which they apply. This is called the **principle of inheritance**. For example, "lays eggs" is a property of all BIRDS, and is thus attached to the BIRDS level, not to the ANIMAL level (as not all animals lay eggs). The principle of inheritance dictates that any feature stored at one level (BIRDS) applies to all the lower-level concepts in the hierarchy. Properties more specific to each kind of bird are then stored at the subordinate level: robins, but not ostriches, have a red breast; ostriches, but not robins, are large.

When people are asked to verify sentences such as "A robin is a bird" or "A robin is an animal," the amount of time to verify the sentence is based on the number of nodes, or the semantic distance that must be traveled. Thus, confirming that a robin is a bird (1 level away) should be faster than verifying that a robin is an animal (2 levels away). Likewise, verifying that robins have certain properties will be a function of semantic distance, as well—it will be fastest to verify that a robin has a red breast, second fastest verify that it lays eggs (stored at BIRDS level), and slowest to verify that robins breathe (stored at ANIMALS level).

other finding from sentence verifications tasks is the **typicality effect**— more typical or common instances of a category ("A robin is a bird") are responded to more quickly than atypical or uncommon instances ("An ostrich a bird"). For this reason, Collins (with Loftus, 1975) later proposed t a better way to conceptualize category knowledge is through a **spreading activation network**: related concepts (Bird, Robin, Ostrich) are attached, h the strength of the attachment based on the strength of the relationship Thus, Robin, as a more common exemplar of the category BIRD, will l a stronger connection in this network, and thus be verified more quickly his network also allows some activation to spread to related concepts. If you verify "A robin is a bird," some activation will spread to other BIRDS, and you should be a little faster to then verify that "An ostrich is a bird" than someone who hadn't received the ROBIN statement first. Spreading activation models can also explain some of the effects in the Lexical Decision ZAP.

ZAPS: SENTENCE VERIFICATION

Questions

1. Since typical and nontypical instances of a category (ROBIN; OSTRICH) are stored at the same level in Collins and Quillian's model, how can they explain the typicality effect?

2. Why might a spreading activation network be more flexible for representing, say, connections among your friends or other categories that can't easily be put into a hierarchy?

ZAPS | Serial Position Task

> **How to:** You will be presented with a list of 12 words, one at a time, which you are to try to remember as best you can. You will then be asked to recall the words (in any order, but be sure to spell the words correctly). This will be repeated for 4 additional memory trials of 12 words each.

Many factors determine what we remember: Common words are more easily retrieved than rare words, events that are meaningful to us are better remembered than mundane events, words that are easy to image (*raccoon*) are more easily recalled than words that aren't easy to image (*freedom*). But another reason that an item may be remembered has nothing to do with the word or item itself, but where it appears in a list. This is known as the **serial position effect**—memory is dependent on the serial position of a stimulus in a list.

For instance, we know that the first few items in a list *and* the last few items tend to be best remembered (though for very different reasons). The tendency to recall the first few items in a list is known as the **primacy effect**; the tendency to recall the first few items in a list is called the **recency effect** (since those were the most recent words to which you were exposed before recalling them).

The recency effect is easy to explain—the last items in a list are still in short-term memory, and thus easily retrieved. The primacy effect, though, is due to better processing of the initial items in a list, so that they are more likely to get into longer-term memory. Researchers have determined that if there is a delay between presentation of a list of words and when a person is asked to recall them, the primacy effect is maintained, but the recency effect disappears (since the items are no longer in short-term store).

179

Rundus and Atkinson asked subjects to rehearse out loud as they tried to remember a list of words. They found (a) the initial words in the list were rehearsed most, and (b) the number of rehearsals was highly correlated with the primary and middle items in a list (with the early words getting the most rehearsal and the highest likelihood of being recalled). However, the recency items did not get many rehearsals, and yet were well-remembered, indicating that the recency effect is due to a different cognitive mechanism than the primacy effect.

ZAPS: SERIAL POSITION TASK

Questions

1. Do you think that the serial position effect would occur if you tried to remember items over a longer-term basis—such as all the friends you encountered in a single day on campus, or all the tasks/errands you ran? What other factors might be more important than serial position in your memory for friends or errands?

2. What memory strategies did you find yourself using during the ZAP experiment? Was rehearsal one of the strategies? Were you able to fit in more rehearsals for early items?

ZAPS | Signal Detection

HOW TO: Press the **Start** button to see the first suspect. Pay very careful attention to the suspect's features, as this is the person you will try to detect in 43 lineups. Press the **space bar** to see the first line-up. Press the **m**-key if the suspect you originally saw is present in the line-up; the **c**-key if he is not present. There is no time limit. Three practice lineups will be followed by 40 test lineups (the same suspect must be detected in all lineups).

You decide to make some spare money in the summer by becoming a baseball umpire for Little League. "Better than flipping burgers," you reason. You spend 12 hours in a training course on the rules of baseball, and how to tell the difference between a pitch that is a strike and a non-strike. Of course, there are some pitches that are hard to judge, but you assume you'll get better over time.

Your first hired game is on a balmy Wednesday night. As you get out of your car, eager to test your newly formed umpire skills, a man on crutches with a broken leg, broken nose, and a black eye summons you over. He tells you that he was last week's umpire at this field, and warns you about the hometown crowd here. The Little League parents are a little overzealous, he states, and roughed him up a bit after some controversial pitching calls.

Assuming you seek self-preservation, you're in a bit of a dilemma. Although you vow to remain objective, when the home team (with the violent parents) is pitching, you find your criteria for a strike are rather liberal. Even when you're unsure whether a pitch is a strike or a ball, you tend to favor, "*Strike!*" However, when the other team is pitching to the home team, you find your criteria for what constitutes a strike to be conservative; any uncertain pitches are categorized as non-strikes (or balls).

In this example, discerning strike pitches from non-strike (or ball) pitches is really just a signal detection task, analogous to a radar detector trying to separate bleeps on the radar screen that indicate that airplanes are in the vicinity from those that indicate flocks of birds. There are 4 potential options in a signal detection task:

1. **Hit:** A target *is* present, and you detect it. That is, you call a strike a strike.
2. **Miss:** A target *is* present, but you *don't* detect it. You miscall an actual strike, and call it a ball.
3. **Correct Rejection:** A target *is not* present, and you claim nothing was detected. In other words, you correctly call a ball a ball.
4. **False Alarm:** A target *is not* present, but you claim you saw a target. You call an actual ball a strike.

Whether you are an umpire judging strike balls, or someone watching a radar screen, it is your job to detect a *signal.* Some stimuli will be easy to judge as a target (a pitch dead center in the strike zone); others will be easy to judge as a non-target (a pitch that veers straight over the batter's head). Other stimuli will require more of a judgment call (a pitch that enters the bottom corner of a strike zone). Thus, aspects of the stimuli themselves (e.g., the location of a pitch) influence our signal detection accuracy.

Psychological factors, though, also influence signal detection. For example, your fear about being beat up by the home-team Little League parents leads you to be liberal when the home team is pitching (leading to more false alarms), but conservative when the other team is pitching (resulting in more misses). This is not necessarily a strategy of which you are conscious (though it turns out to prevent you from sustaining bodily damage). The Signal Detection Theory is based on the knowledge that our judgments about whether a stimulus is present or not is a function of both the physical aspects of the stimulus and the psychological qualities and strategies of the person performing the judgments.

ZAPS: SIGNAL DETECTION

Questions

1. What ordinary ventures might count as signal detection tasks? Name at least 3 such tasks you might encounter in a week.

2. Think of a navy recruit being trained in signal detection. What psychological factors (e.g., anxiety) might influence his or her accuracy?

| Signal Detection II

How to: It is highly recommended that you do the first Signal Detection ZAP (Signal Detection Theory) before attempting this ZAP. The **Start** button begins each trial. Based on what you learned in the first signal detection ZAP, drag the labels in the box at the top of each screen to the correct oblong areas in the graph below. Be sure to position the labels carefully so that your answers will count as correct. Click **Check** for feedback about your answer. You may make multiple attempts on each assignment. When you are correct, the **Continue** button will appear. Click it to go to the next problem. There are 14 assignments in all.

Psychophysics is the study of how we psychologically process physical stimuli, and derive a mathematical relationship between an auditory, visual, or tactile stimulus and what we hear, see, or feel. Much of the historical work in psychophysics, dating back to the German researchers von Helmholtz, Weber, and Fechner, focused on finding the **absolute threshold** for people's detection of physical stimuli. In other words, how strong does a stimulus have to be before we can detect it at least half the time? For instance, the absolute threshold for vision is being able to see a candle in the clear dark at 30 miles; for hearing it is the tick of a clock 20 feet away in otherwise silent conditions. Initially, it was thought that detection of a stimulus was **all or none—** at a certain frequency, you will hear auditory information; beneath that level you will not. It is now known that we detect stimuli in degrees. There are some sounds we will never be able to hear (e.g., a dog whistle, bat sonar), and others we can't help but hear (e.g., our neighbor's stereo when she blares heavy metal music). But much of the auditory stimuli in between these two extremes will be unevenly detected.

One technique for studying stimulus detection is a **forced choice technique**—a stimulus of a given strength (e.g., concentration of sugar in a gallon of pure water) is presented, and a subject needs to decide whether she detects the stimulus or not. Let's say Alicia can detect a teaspoon of sugar in a gallon of water 50% of the time, but a half teaspoon of sugar only 20% of the time. If we continue to vary the concentration of sugar in a gallon of water, we will be able to chart the sugar concentration along the x-axis, and the percentage of time she detects that concentration along the y-axis.

What this graph would show is that Alicia's probability of detecting sugar in water is a function of the strength of the stimulus (the sugar concentration). But, this may not be the only factor in Alicia's detecting a sweet taste to water; her judgments of whether sugar is present in water or not is also dependent on psychological factors. **Signal Detection Theory** is based on the notion that whenever one is trying to detect a stimulus, there will always be a certain degree of random noise, and that detecting a stimulus involves *judgments* of whether that stimulus is easily separable from such noise. For example, if you are viewing a candle 30 miles away in dark, clear conditions, it may not always be evident that you have detected a candle rather than the random light flashes you sometimes "see" in the dark (due to random firing of neurons).

Stimuli, and sometimes noise, cause an **internal response** in your sensory system. The stronger the stimulus, the larger the internal response. For unclear cases that cause weaker internal responses, a person must decide whether he or she has seen (or heard or tasted . . .) a stimulus or not. Some of this will be based on a person's **criterion** for saying "yes." Conservative people may be unwilling to make false alarms (see the Signal Detection ZAP for basic information on signal detection theory), and thus have more "no" responses (even when a stimulus was present). Those with liberal criteria may prefer false alarms to misses, and thus "yes" responses may predominate (even when *no* stimulus was present).

Signal detection theory states that people may have differential **sensitivity** to stimuli (conveyed by d′); some people can hear weaker sounds than others, and a single person may detect weak sounds better one day than another. This sensitivity can be mathematically calculated for a person under a given set of conditions, and then charted on a receiver-operating-characteristic curve (or ROC curve for short). See the ROC curve in the "Further Information" section of the ZAP.

The ROC curve depicts the rate of false alarms (x-axis) to misses (y-axis). When d′ = 0, this shows that a person's sensitivity to whether a stimulus is present or not is not very accurate, and akin to pure guessing. A student who has just pulled two all-nighters to write a term paper may be highly inaccurate at seeing the candlelight at 30 miles away. The higher the d′ score, the more sensitive a person is about detecting when a stimulus is present or not. The same student, after catching up on sleep, may become very sensitive to seeing the candlelight at 30 miles away, and also be able to detect when his eyes might be playing a visual trick on him.

ZAPS: SIGNAL DETECTION II

Questions

1. What physical and psychological factors are likely to influence a person's sensitivity to a stimulus?

2. Do you think training in a signal detection task would be able to increase a person's sensitivity? Why or why not?

ZAPS | Simon Effect

> **HOW TO:** It's important to keep your left index finger on the
> c-key and your right index finger on the **m**-key throughout this
> entire experiment. Focus your eyes on the fixation dot in the mid-
> dle of the screen. Every time you see an orange square, press
> the c-key; every time you see a blue square, press the **m**-key. Try
> to be as quick and accurate as possible.

Imagine walking into a foyer with an umbrella stand on the right and a key
hook on the left. You are holding your keys in your right hand and your
umbrella in your left. What is the likelihood that you hang up your umbrella and drop your keys in the umbrella stand? Do you think you'd be
more accurate if you entered with your umbrella in your right hand (same
side as the umbrella stand) and your keys in your left (same side as the key
hook)? The Simon effect predicts that you would.

In the lab, as in real life, people are faster and more accurate at responding to stimuli in the same spatial location as the response key. In other
words, response times to left-hand stimuli are fastest if you respond with
your left hand and fastest to right-hand stimuli if you respond with your
right hand. This holds true for responding to blue versus orange squares
(as in the ZAP demonstration), for signaling right-hand turns when the
signal indicator is on the right-hand side of the steering wheel, or for putting away objects when they are in hands that are consonant to the containers
in which they are to be placed.

Researchers have determined that there are 3 main stages to the Simon
effect–style task:

1. **Stimulus identification:** You identify that you hold keys and an
   umbrella in your hands.

2. **Response selection:** You determine that you want to put away the umbrella and the keys. However, at this stage there may be two competing responses: (1) keys go on the key ring; umbrella in the umbrella stand, versus (2) deposit the keys and umbrella on the same side in which you are holding them.
3. **Execution of the response:** Actually hanging up one item on the key ring and dropping the other in the umbrella stand.

The Simon effect is thought to be due to the interference at the Response selection stage. Even if you successfully locate your keys on the key ring and your umbrella in the umbrella stand, it will take *longer* (due to response competition) when you are holding the items on the wrong sides.

The Simon effect is one of many factors that people who design machines must consider, especially when there are safety issues. Imagine how confused (and accident-prone) we all would be if steering wheels were designed to turn in the *opposite* direction from which you wished to turn. There might even be accidents if we had to push a steering wheel *up* in order to turn right, and push it *down* to turn left. The time and accuracy of responses are highest when the responses mirror the spatial location of the items to which we are attending.

Designing machines that adhere to the Simon principle is referred to as human-machine interface. There are other factors that engineers who design machines need to think about. It is not enough to design an efficient machine if the people who use it make many mistakes (even potentially fatal mistakes). For example, Kendler (1987) reported on a World War II airplane that led many pilots to land the planes on their bellies. Why? The braking lever and the landing-gear lever were right next to each other, so pilots would attempt to brake, only to mistakenly retract the landing wheels.

ZAPS: SIMON EFFECT

Questions

1. Why is the interference in the Simon effect not at the level of stimulus identification? Why isn't it at the level of response execution?

2. What types of machines and programs adhere to the Simon principle? What violations of human-machine interface can you find in machines that we use every day (e.g., is it a design flaw to have the accelerator and brake pedals so close to each other in cars)?

ZAPS | Spatial Cueing

How to: At the beginning of each trial, a fixation point will appear in the center of the screen. Focus your attention on the fixation point. The fixation point will then be replaced either with an arrow ($\rightarrow$ or $\leftarrow$), or with a + sign. On the arrow trials, 80% of the time, the arrow accurately indicates the correct location of a red square that will be presented. The other 20% of the time, the arrow points in the wrong direction. On the neutral + trials, there is an equal likelihood that the square will appear on the left or the right. Push the **m**-key as quickly as possible when you see the red square. You will be given feedback after each trial. You will have 3 practice trials, then 60 actual trials.

The outdoor concert at which you are to meet your roommate is crowded with people. You scan the crowd for your friend's distinctive lime-green jacket, but without success. However, you then remember that your friend said he would stand by the concession stand. You look in that direction, and immediately find your friend.

Assuming no one else in the crowd was wearing the same loudly colored jacket, why was it easier to find your friend when you shifted your attention to the concession stand? Some researchers have termed this the **spotlight metaphor** of visual attention—when focusing your attention is like shining a spotlight on one particular item. We can then move the spotlight around at will until we find what we are looking for (in this case, our friend). Processing information within that attentional spotlight will be faster and more accurate than processing information that is not highlighted by the spotlight. The spatial cueing effect is a good example of this.

Your friend's hint that he would stand over by the concession stands is a **spatial cue**—it allows you to direct your attention and your gaze toward a particular spatial location within the concert. This hint then increases the probability of your finding your friend. Likewise, the time it takes to find your friend is less than it would be if you didn't receive a spatial cue.

Posner first proposed the spotlight metaphor of visual attention. He also claimed that visual attention can shift independently of eye movement; that is, your attention can change even if your eyes stay still. An example of this is the pop-up advertisements that you see when you surf the Web. Your eyes may be stationary on the computer screen, but your attention is diverted when a bright pop-up advertisement for stereo equipment appears in the bottom right-hand corner of your screen.

ZAPS: SPATIAL CUEING

Questions

1. List 3 real-life instances of spatial cueing.

2. Intuitively, does the spotlight metaphor of visual attention seem like a good analogy? What does it predict about our ability to process information that is not within the spotlight? Does it make sense to distinguish the spotlight's center from its periphery?

ZAPS | Split Brain

> **How to:** For each trial, choose an object (apple, mug, keys) and whether the word corresponding to that object (e.g., "apple") will be presented to the left or right visual field, and which hand the patient should use to retrieve the object from behind the screen. Press the **Start** button to begin. The pathway that the information takes to the brain will be shown, as well as the split-brain patient's behavioral and potential verbal response. To start a new trial, choose a different set of object/visual field/hand. Be sure to try a number of combinations to best learn how a split-brain patient would perform in such a task.

Despite popular books such as *Drawing on the Right Side of Your Brain* and pop psychology quizzes about whether you are more right-brained or more left-brained, most skills we have are accomplished by the cooperation of our right and left hemispheres. However, sometimes one hemisphere is *better* at a skill than the other. The tendency for the two hemispheres to be differentially specialized is known as **lateralization**. This concept was recognized even in ancient times; Galen, a Greek physician who treated some of the injured gladiators in Rome, realized that the gladiators were most likely to suffer language impairments after a blow to the left side of the skull. However, lateralization did not become fully respectable in scientific circles until 1861, when Paul Broca reported that an aphasic patient of his had brain damage in the front left cerebral cortex.

There are several ways to study which skills are better in the left versus the right hemisphere: like Broca or Galen, we can wait for someone to suffer a stroke on one side of the brain and see which abilities are disrupted. Or, we can measure brain activity in each hemisphere while someone performs a language, or a piece of music, or a visual task (e.g., by using a PET scan).

A third way is to study split-brain patients, whose main bundle of neurons that allow the left and right hemispheres to communicate, has been severed. Why would anyone elect to have the corpus callosum—the main bundle of axons permitting information to pass back and forth between the left to right hemisphere—cut? Often, these are people who suffer from severe epilepsy that is not lessened by drugs. The split-brain operation prevents the overzealous electrical activity during an epileptic seizure from spreading to the opposite hemisphere. Aside from the surgery itself, and some competition between the two halves of the body, there are few side effects from the split-brain operation (one patient reported that, as one hand was buttoning a shirt, the other would be unbuttoning).

A fact relevant to the study of brain lateralization is that people who suffer a left-hemisphere stroke are often paralyzed on the right side of the body. The brain has **contralateral** control (opposite-side control of the body). And what about seeing—does information from each eye get processed by the opposite hemisphere? No; it turns out the truth is a little more complicated. Instead, each *visual field* is processed contralaterally. Information presented to the *left* visual field goes to both eyes, but largely ends up in the *right* visual cortex (in the occipital lobe). The opposite is true for information presented to the *right* visual field.

In normal subjects, any information that was presented to the left visual field and made its way to the right hemisphere would quickly be shared with the left hemisphere through connections in the corpus callosum. With split-brain patients, it is easier to isolate information to either hemisphere, because the two sides of the brain can't share information. Scientists such as Michael Gazzaniga and Roger Sperry studied some of the first split-brain patients extensively. For example, in one experiment, they flashed words to either the LVF (processed by the right hemisphere) or the RVF (processed by the left hemisphere). They found that the patients were *most* likely to be able to say the word out loud when it was flashed to the RVF, though some patients could *identify* the object named by a word—*keys*—even when flashed to the LVF. This shows that the right hemisphere has some language comprehension, even if it is not good at pronouncing words. In another trial, the researchers flashed a picture (e.g., *hammer*) to either the RVF or LVF and asked split-brain patients to feel around for the object depicted behind a screen in which there were an array of objects (hammer, book, cup). If a picture of a hammer appeared in the LVF, the subject's right hemisphere could process this information, and then send a message to the left hand to retrieve the item from behind the screen.

As illustrated in the ZAP demonstration, clever experiments such as those conducted with split-brain patients have allowed insight into lateralization—the different specializations of the two hemispheres. It has allowed us to know that the right hemisphere is better at visual-spatial skills, especially at detecting "whole" patterns, and that the left hemisphere is more detail-oriented and language based (confirming what Galen and Broca reported hundreds and thousands of years earlier).

ZAPS: SPLIT BRAIN

Questions

1. A split-brain patient sees *clap* flashed to the LVF and *laugh* flashed to the RVF simultaneously. What does she verbally report that she saw? Does she behaviorally respond to both cues, and why (or why not)?

2. Why do you think we evolved differential specializations of the two hemispheres? What advantage would that give us for survival, or in competition for resources with other animals?

3. Do you consider yourself more of a right-brain or a left-brain person? Why? Have you ever taken an online test that purports to tell you whether you are right- or left-brain dominant? How accurate is this assessment, based on what you now know?

How to: In each trial, 2 categories (e.g., Man, Woman) will appear in the upper-right and -left corners. On the bottom of the screen, in the middle, a word will appear (e.g., Jane). Decide whether the word is more associated with the category in the left-hand corner (Man) or with the category in the right-hand corner (Woman). Press the **c**-key if the center word is associated with the left-hand category, or press the **m**-key if the word is associated with the right-hand category. Be as quick but as accurate as possible.

If your response is wrong (e.g., you associate "Jane" with "Man"), the word will reappear. There are 100 trials broken down into 7 sections. *Read the beginning of each section carefully, as the types of categories to which you will be responding change with each section.* Your data will appear at the end.

There is an old riddle: A man and his father are in a car accident. The man is rushed to the hospital for surgery. As he is wheeled into the emergency room, the doctor says, "I can't operate on him; this is my son."

Most of us, if asked, would claim that we are not sexist, and believe in equal opportunities for men and women. However, it takes us a few more seconds to figure out that riddle than if the riddle read: ". . . the nurse says . . ." Why? When we hear the word "doctor" we automatically assume that the doctor is a male, and then have to rethink that the doctor is a female (and the man's mother) so that the joke makes sense. This is a difference between our **explicit attitudes** and our **implicit attitudes**—at a conscious (or explicit) level, we are not sexist and believe that both men and women make competent doctors. However, at an unconscious (or implicit) level, we associate "doctors" more with men than with women.

The **implicit attitudes test** was developed by Mahzarin Banaji. Its basic premise is that the speed with which we respond to the association between two categories (e.g., woman-gossip) is an indication of unconscious (or implicit) beliefs or feelings. For example, we may explicitly state that we think men and women are equally likely to gossip, but unconsciously believe that women are more likely to gossip. There are several versions of the IAT designed to explore the difference in implicit and explicit attitudes regarding race, ethnicity, sex/gender, sexual orientation, age, and body image (fat/thin).

Stereotyping is the tendency to infer certain properties on people who belong to a given category, such as inferring that doctors are most likely male. The 2 major problems with stereotypes are accuracy and negative evaluations. The tendency to categorize is a strong human characteristic. It saves us valuable time when we can use category membership to make useful inferences—the banana in our lunch will taste good because most other bananas taste good; the smiling person on the street will help give us directions because smiling people are usually helpful. Sometimes, even religion-based, or race-based, or gender-based stereotyping will be accurate: Catholics *are* more likely to oppose abortion than are Protestants; Asian-Americans (on average) do score higher on standardized math tests, and the American Medical Association reports that there are 3 male physicians for every 1 female physician. However, not all stereotypes are universally accurate within the category (pediatricians are as likely to be female as male, with female numbers climbing), nor are they necessarily accurate when applied to a single individual (some bananas taste bad, some Catholics support reproductive rights, and an individual Asian-American may lament that his math scores are not excellent).

The other downfall to stereotyping is that it leads to negative evaluations of individuals within a group that may translate into prejudicial behavior. For example, the financial aid officer who implicitly believes that men make better doctors may give more money to male medical students. Or the teacher who implicitly believes that females are worse at math than males, but Asian-Americans who are superior to others at math, may not sufficiently challenge the females and may ignore an Asian-American student who needs extra math help. The IAT seeks to make us more aware of our underlying stereotypes and potential prejudices, so that we can do something to change them.

However, some critics have argued that the response times in IAT are longer for unfamiliar categories, not because of any underlying prejudice (Brendl, Markman, & Messner, 2001). In other words, an Asian-American might respond slower to "Black-intelligent" than to "White-intelligent" simply because they are not as familiar with black people (rather than because they have implicit racial stereotypes). The IAT's supporters admit that familiarity influences the test's results, but that it is still valid for measuring unconscious attitudes (Ottaway, Hayden, & Oakes, 2001).

ZAPS: STEREOTYPES

Questions

1. Which of the implicit attitudes tests (on race, ethnicity, sex/gender, sexual orientation, age, and body image (fat/thin)) do you think would reveal the biggest discrepancy between your explicit and your implicit attitudes?

2. Why is it useful to know about our implicit attitudes? Wouldn't it be more comfortable not to know that we have residual stereotypes about gender or race or age? What can we do to make our implicit and explicit attitudes more consistent with each other?

ZAPS | Sternberg Search

How to: On each trial, you will be presented with 1, 3, or 5 capital letters. This is the **memory set**. Then, a probe, or **target item**, will appear. As quickly as possible, press the **c**-key if the probe was NOT in the original memory set, or the **m**-key if the probe was in the original memory set. Remember, speed of response is important in this experiment. There are 3 practice trials, then 60 experimental trials.

We have already seen that short-term memory (or the more contemporary *working memory*) has a limited capacity. However, once we have that small amount of information temporarily stored, how do we scan it to determine what information has been maintained? In this experiment, you see a memory set of 1, 3, or 5 items. Then a probe appears, and you have to determine whether that probe (or target item) had appeared in the memory set.

Saul Sternberg first conducted this experiment, and claimed that there were 3 possibilities for how we scan STM (short-term memory):

1. All items of the memory set are searched simultaneously, in what is called a **parallel search**. If this is the case, searching for the probe in a memory set of 1 should not differ from a memory set of 3, or a memory set of 5. As we have seen, this is not the case.
2. Items in the scanned array are searched one at a time (a *serial* search) *until* the correct one is found (a *self-terminating* search). If a **serial, self-terminating search** is initiated, then search times should be shorter if the probe was the second item in the memory set versus the fourth item in the memory set. Sternberg did not find that this is the case.
3. Items in the scanned array are searched one at a time, but the scan continues to the last item, *even if* the correct item has already been

found. If this is true, then scanning times should be correlated with the number of items in a memory set (but not with where the item is located in the memory set). Sternberg called this a **serial, exhaustive search**. He found the most support for this position; each item added to the memory set increased test response times by an average of 38 milliseconds.

Why would we continue scanning a memory set, even after the probe has been detected? After all, if you are searching for a book on your bookshelf, you would stop when you found it and wouldn't continue searching the rest of the shelf. Sternberg hypothesized that there may actually be 2 stages to STM scanning: the scanning itself, and the double-check to make sure that one's response is correct. It is more time efficient to fully scan the array and then double-check the response than it is to scan each item *and* double-check it one at a time. Perhaps this analogy will help: Imagine that you needed to make 25 copies of a double-sided document. The most efficient way for the photocopier to do this is to make 25 copies of the first side, flip all the pages and then make 25 copies of page 2 on the reverse side. This is analogous to scanning and then double-checking before making a response, as in a serial, exhaustive search. Imagine how much longer it would take if the machine made a copy of side 1, flipped that page and made a copy of side 2, then moved on to the next page—side 1, flip, side 2, then the next page—side 1, flip, side 2 . . . and so on for 25 pages (similar to scanning and double-checking each item in a memory set).

ZAPS: STERNBERG SEARCH

Questions

1. Can you think of any other endeavors in which a serial, exhaustive search would be useful? When could we realistically conduct a parallel search?

2. Do you think that subjects would continue to use a serial, exhaustive search if the size of the memory set were increased to 7 items? To 10 items?

3. If you had to scan a picture you had in memory to determine whether an object was depicted in the scene (e.g., was there a rabbit in the picture of a forest scene?), would the same scanning principles apply as when Sternberg used verbal-type stimuli (letters)? Why or why not?

Stroop Effect

> **How to:** Press the **Start** button to begin. Pay attention to the white square in the middle of the screen; this is where each stimulus will appear. Your task is to respond based on the color ink in which the stimulus word is printed (not on the basis of the word itself). Press the **r**-key for red, the **b**-key for blue, and the **g**-key for green. You will be given feedback after each trial as to whether you were correct or incorrect. There are 5 practice trials, then 45 test trials.

When you first learned to ride a 2-wheeled bicycle, it was a laborious process. One of your parents had to stand alongside you, holding the bicycle steady while you tried to pedal. When your parents were confident enough to let go of you, it is likely that you fell several times. You may have found that having to pay attention to pedaling, keeping your balance, and watching out for objects in front of you all at the same time was very difficult.

How, then, do you find riding a bicycle so effortless now? Even if you don't ride your bicycle for several months—such as during the winter—when you get back on, you find yourself skilled at bicycle riding. You might also notice that you don't deliberately pay attention to pedaling, or keeping yourself upright—it just seems to happen.

Many skills that start out as difficult can become automatic. Word Recognition is one such skill. In first grade, reading may have been a laborious process as you struggled to sound words out or recognize them from the context in the book. By college, you have read so much that recognition of most words is automatic. In fact, if you are told *not* to recognize the meaning of the word below, it will be difficult to obey this command:

VACATION

Skills that have become automatic use up less attentional capacity. When you were age 6, reading the word *vacation* would have taken you several seconds as you worked through the phonetics of the word. Furthermore, your beginning skill level would have required that you focus intently on the reading process (and it would have required much of your attentional capacity). Now, over 10 years since you first learned to read, ***semantic activation*** of the word *vacation* is instantaneous and seemingly automatic. It also doesn't require much attentional capacity—you know what the word means even if you glance at it while your roommate is occupying most of your attention.

The Stroop task illustrates that a previously effortful process can become automatic with sufficient practice (like bike-riding or reading). J. Ridley Stroop introduced this task in a 1935 paper. Findings usually conclude that:

- Naming colors takes longer than reading words. Why? Your responses in the Stroop Task are verbal. Printed words are already in a form that causes you to access a verbal response, "blue," directly. When you look at a color, there is an additional step to retrieve the verbal label for that color, which may add a second or 2 or 3 to your naming score.
- When reading words, the color ink that the word is printed in typically causes very little interference. In other words, people usually take about as much time to read words in black and white as they do to read words in color ink (even when the color ink—green—is different from the word they are reading, *red*).

The Stroop Effect usually refers to the much greater interference (longer times) needed to name color inks (e.g., green ink) when that ink is used to spell out a non-corresponding color word (as when the word *red* is printed in that green ink). It is a clever way to illustrate how a skill that has become automatic can cause interfere in a secondary task that is not automatic (such as color naming). In the same way, if you were asked to quickly name the number of items in an array, which would be quicker and easier?

X X X

or

5 5 5

Presumably, the three Xs would enable a quick response, whereas recognizing the 5s would interfere with your saying that there are three items.

Hasher and Zacks (1979, 1984) claimed that one way to test whether a skill has become automatic is if you can engage in it and still have plenty of attention left for another task. For example, many people find that driving initially requires so much attentional capacity that changing the radio station or having a conversation leads to driving errors. A few years practice, though, and people find it easier to have conversations while driving (as long as traffic isn't too bad).

ZAPS: STROOP EFFECT

Questions

1. What do you think would happen if the color words were printed in a language that you did not understand; would you show longer response times due to interference? What if a French-English bilingual person were to see French color words while they were naming the color inks in English? Would there be more or less interference if they were to name the color ink in French (if the color names were also printed in French)?

2. What are some other skills that started out effortful, and became more automatic? What is the evidence that these skills are now automatic?

Syllogisms

How to: You will be presented with 5 syllogisms, each of which consists of 2 premises (P1 and P2) and a conclusion. Your task is to judge the validity of each argument—does the conclusion necessarily follow from the premises?

If I don't pay my phone bill, my phone will be turned off.
I didn't pay my phone bill.
Therefore, my phone will be turned off.

Some professors are female.
Some professors are male.
Therefore, some females are male.

In deductive reasoning, arguments are made up of statements known as premises, and then a conclusion. When an argument is valid, the conclusion logically follows from the premises (as in the phone bill argument above). When the argument is invalid, the conclusion does not necessarily follow from the premises (as in the professor argument above). Notice that nothing has been said about *truth*; arguments are not judged based on their truth but on their **validity**. For example:

Unicorns eat hay.
All animals who eat hay are real.
Therefore, unicorns are real.

Now we know that unicorns are fictitious animals, and so the conclusion, "Therefore, unicorns are real," might make us think that the argument is invalid because we don't believe the conclusion (based on what we know to be true). Actually, the argument is *valid* because the conclusion does follow logically from the premises. What the problem is about—its content—does not influence the validity of the argument. Experts and logicians know this. However, the content of a problem clearly influences *judgments* that regular people (non-logicians) might make about arguments. Logicians understand that the unicorn argument is logically valid; we might conclude that since unicorns are not real, then the argument is invalid. But we would be wrong.

This ZAP illustrates to you how problem content can deter us from making correct assessments of the validity of arguments. One way to improve our reasoning skills is through the use of Euler diagrams, which is also illustrated in this ZAP Discovery.

ZAPS: SYLLOGISMS

Questions

1. Why do you think we are so influenced by the content of problems? Do you think being influenced by content might actually be an adaptive way to reason in real life?

2. Why do diagrams (such as Euler diagrams) help us determine whether an argument is logically valid?

3. How might taking a class in logic to learn what constitutes a valid argument, and which kinds of arguments are fallacies, help you in assessing advertising and medical claims?

> **How to:** In this ZAP, you will follow the neural pathway of a message (such as when a person burns his or her finger). Continue to click on each of the buttons as they appear beneath the gray bar at the bottom of the page. You will then see each step, have the ability to zoom in on some of the neural processes, and receive explanations about action potentials, how neural messages are passed on, and the effects of drugs and tranquilizers on neural messages.

Historically, there have been many explanations—both reasonable and outlandish—for how we are able to remember information, make our arm raise at will, feel cold. For example, a popular view in the seventeenth century was the Hydraulic theory of movement, based on the mechanisms of garden statues. If a person desired to move her arm, a crucial part of the brain would tip, allowing fluid from the ventricles of the brain to flow down into the arm, causing it to move. We now know that the truth is more complicated and more elegant than that. Neurons, by passing their messages on to muscles, or to other neurons, are responsible for detecting messages from the body, causing our motor movements, and storing memories.

How can these specialized cells do all this? The process by which a neuron passes a message within itself, from the dendrites to the axon, is known as **conduction**. The process by which one neuron passes its message to a second neuron is **transmission**. Transmission is accomplished when chemicals, known as neurotransmitters, are released from synaptic vesicles in the bottom of axons of the first (presynaptic) neuron, across the synapse (the microscopic gap between neurons), to the second (postsynaptic) neuron.

Neurotransmitters can be either excitatory or inhibitory: if excitatory, they make the postsynaptic neuron *more* likely to fire; if inhibitory, they make the postsynaptic neuron *less* likely to fire. Each neurotransmitter is like a key that only "unlocks" specific receptors on postsynaptic neurons (in the same way that your car starts your car but not your neighbor's). When released into the synaptic gap, the receptors on the postsynaptic cell will detect the neurotransmitter, and cause an excitatory or inhibitory response in the postsynaptic neuron.

There are 15 to 20 chemicals known to be neurotransmitters, and many more that are suspected of being neurotransmitters. One such neurotransmitter is **acetylcholine**, which helps send messages from neurons to your muscles to enable you to turn the pages of this manual, or press the computer keys when you respond in the ZAP experiments, or walk from one class to another. When it synapses onto muscles, it acts as an excitatory neurotransmitter. Another prevalent neurotransmitter is **dopamine**, which helps control both voluntary muscle movements, pleasurable emotions, and some perceptual abilities. Too little dopamine (because of death of the neurons that produce it) leads to the jerky, uncontrollable motions in Parkinson's disease. Overuse of dopamine is thought to underlie the emotional abnormalities and hallucinations of schizophrenics. A third well-known neurotransmitter is **serotonin**, which plays a role in sleep/wake cycles, positive mood, and inhibition of aggressive behavior. Depressed people, for example, often have too little serotonin in their system (which may also account for why they suffer from irregular sleep patterns).

Many drugs and poisons work by acting on a specific neurotransmitter. Drugs or substances that *enhance* the effect of a neurotransmitter are called **agonists**; those that prevent the effectiveness of a neurotransmitter are called **antagonists**. For instance, anti-depressant drugs such as Prozac are agonists of serotonin—they allow more serotonin to remain in the synaptic gap, thus increasing the person's positive mood. Agonists can work in a variety of ways—by causing the release of more neurotransmitter, or preventing the recycling of excess neurotransmitter back into the presynaptic neuron (this is one of the ways that Prozac works). Antagonists can also work in a variety of ways—by blocking the receptor sites for the neurotransmitter on the postsynaptic cell (as when antipsychotic drugs given to schizophrenics block the receptors for dopamine), or by increasing the reuptake (or recycling) of the neurotransmitter (Lithium given to manic-depressive patients increases reuptake of the neurotransmitter norepinephrine).

The electrical process of sending a neural message is influenced by the excitatory or inhibitory nature of the neurotransmitter. Excitatory neurotransmitters cause channels in the postsynaptic neuron to open, which make the electrical charge inside the cell *more* positive. If the change is sufficiently more positive, and achieves that neuron's **threshold**, an **action potential** will occur. This allows the message to be conducted down the length of the neuron, and passed on to yet another postsynaptic neuron. Inhibitory neurotransmitters cause channels in the postsynaptic neuron to close, thereby leading to more of a negative charge. The neuron is then said to be **hyperpolarized**, and less likely to achieve action potential.

ZAPS: SYNAPTIC TRANSMISSION

Questions

1. During surgery, children (and some adults) are given not only anesthetic, but also amnesic-type drugs so that they don't remember the surgery. How do you think these amnesic drugs work at the level of synaptic transmission?

2. Black widow spider venom is an agonist of acetylcholine; botulism is an antagonist of acetylcholine. Which do you think causes seizures, and which can cause paralysis? Explain why.

3. How do you think scientists are able to identify neurotransmitters and their effects? How does this information help drug companies trying to come up with new chemical cures for many disorders?

HOW TO: Your task is to detect a green circle against a backdrop of other shapes and to press the **m**-key when you detect a green circle, or the **c**-key if you do not detect a green circle on each trial. Make your judgment as quickly and accurately as possible, as all trials are being timed. You will receive feedback after each trial. In part 1 of the experiment, 5 practice trials precede 24 test trials. Read the instructions to part 2 of the experiment carefully before proceeding. You will be permitted 3 practice trials before part 2 begins. Again, in 24 trials, press the **m**-key when you detect a green circle, the **c**-key when you do not detect a green circle.

Where is your favorite T-shirt? After a rough midterm week, you look at the laundry strewn all over your floor and try to find your favorite gray T-shirt, with the logo of your favorite rock band. If you've been wearing gray T-shirts all week (now decorating your floor), this task will be more difficult than if your wardrobe had been colorful African kaftans. The favorite T-shirt is our **target**; the other shirts littering the carpet are the **distracters**. This is the principle behind the visual search task.

When we scan the environment in search of some target, often we might search for one particular feature of the target (e.g., a gray pile indicating our favorite T-shirt). The search is faster and easier if the target stands out in some way from its background. If the other shirts littering the floor are brightly colored kaftans, the gray of the T-shirt will seem to pop automatically out at us. When the distracters share at least one feature with the target, our task becomes more difficult. Then, we must search for conjunctive features (e.g., gray + rock band logo). Now our search seems more deliberate.

Treisman stated that the visual search has two stages—a **preattentive stage** in which individual features (color or shape) are automatically processed (without our needing to "focus" on them), and an **integration stage** in which the conjunction of features are "glued" together into a unified percept. This means that having to pick out a target that differs from its distracters on one dimension, such as shape, should be faster than detecting a target that differs from its distracters on two dimensions. In other words, detecting the letter L in the middle of letter Qs (pre-attentive stage) will be faster and easier than picking out the red L in the midst of red and green Qs (integration stage).

Furthermore, the more distracters in an array, the longer the visual scan time. It will be easier to find your favorite T-shirt if there are only three pieces of clothing on the floor than if there are twelve. The first stage of processing in which individual features of stimuli are recognized involves **illusory conjunctions** in visual search tasks: in busy arrays, people will sometimes report having seen a "red X" in a given location, when what they really saw was a blue X next to a red T. Thus, they must be processing the colors (red, blue) and shapes (X, T) separately, and then confusing which color went with which shape during the integration phase.

When subjects in visual search tasks show illusory conjunctions, they tend to confuse the features of stimuli that are close together. Treisman and Gelade (1980) have argued that this supports the **spotlight analogy of attention** (detailed in the Spatial Cuing ZAP). Being able to accurately represent an object means recognizing that two features co-occur in the same place within space (e.g., with a red X, "redness," and the X-shape are in the same location). People's attention seems to be focused on a given spatial area, so that illusory correlations will be most common with stimuli that are adjacent.

Name: _____

Class: _____

Professor: _____

Date: _____

ZAPS: VISUAL SEARCH

Questions

1. When you scan a crowd for a friend, what features seem most important in helping you to find your friend—his height? hair color? brightly
   colored clothes? unique way of standing? Would your chosen features
   be detected pre-attentively or not?

2. Do you think Treisman's model could be adapted to explain search
   in other modalities—as when we try to locate a friend at a party by
   voice?

> **How to:** You will be presented with 3 logic problems. Read each of them carefully before responding, as the problems may not be as simple as they first appear.

There are 2 main kinds of reasoning:

1. **Inductive reasoning**, where you try to come up with general rules or principles from a set of examples. Chances are that most tigers you've seen in zoos, books, and nature programs are orange and have stripes. Based on your many separate experiences with tigers, it seems safe to infer that the next tiger you see will be orange and have stripes. However, this is not a 100% certainty—you may see a white tiger with black stripes on your next trip to the zoo.
2. **Deductive reasoning**, on the other hand, is geared more toward certainty. Deductive arguments contain premises and a conclusion. The conclusion is deemed valid if it logically follows from the premises. For example,

   > Premise 1: If Jack earns120 credits, he will receive a college degree.
   > Premise 2: Jack earned 120 credits.

   What conclusion seems to naturally follow?

   > Conclusion: Therefore, Jack received a college degree.

This conclusion is guaranteed by the 2 premises. Some premises are couched in "If p, then q" terms (called **conditionals**), similar to the Wason Selection Task. In the above argument, p is "Jack earns 120 credits;" q is "receives a college degree."

The form of that argument is "If p, then q." "P." "Therefore, q." This is a valid argument, because the conclusion logically follows from the premises (and is referred to as **modus ponens**).

What if the second premise was q: Jack received a college degree? Could you reasonably conclude that Jack earned 120 credits? *No.* It is possible that Jack received an honorary degree from a university because he served as their graduation speaker. This argument displays a fallacy known as **Affirming the Consequent.**

What if the second premise was Not P: Jack didn't earn 120 credits? Could you conclude that he didn't receive a college degree? No, for the same reason as above. This fallacy is called **Denying the Antecedent**.

And if the second premise was Not Q: Jack didn't earn a college degree? Could you validly conclude that Jack didn't earn 120 credits? Yes. This is a valid argument (called **modus tollens**).

Let's apply this reasoning to the Wason Selection task. You are to detect whether the rule, "If there is a vowel on one side, then there must be an even number on the other." The 4 options are then an E (p), a K (not-P), a 4 (q) and a 7 (not q). Since the rule clearly applies to the E card, you must turn that over to make sure that there is an even number on the other side (modus ponens). The other card that must be turned over is the 7 (not q), because if there is a vowel on the other side, that card will have violated the rule by having a 7 on its reverse. Why are the other two cards not relevant (and in logical parlance, not valid)? Since the rule doesn't say anything about consonants, it doesn't matter what the K card has on its other side. Furthermore, the 4 card can have either a vowel on the other side (in which the rule applies and is proven true), OR it can have a consonant on the other side (in which case the rule will not apply).

Why, then, do fewer than 10% of people accurately solve the Wason selection task? There are several hypotheses:

1. **Too abstract:** People don't typically think in terms of "If p, then q." Instead they tend to reason based on concrete situations (such as, "If you wash the car, I'll give you $20").
2. **Lack of familiarity:** As can be seen in thise ZAP demo, it is much easier to reason about situations with which we are familiar (such as Griggs and Cox's [1982] drinking problem task). Much research suggests people think more logically if they have had some exposure to the situation about which they are reasoning. Advocates of this view argue that reasoning is domain-specific; we reason well only about specific situations with which we have had experience.
3. **Use of schemata:** People don't think in terms of formal logic, but rather according to a schema they deem relevant to the problem, according to Cheng and Holyoak (1985; Cheng, Holyoak, Nisbett & Oliver, 1986). For instance, if you encounter a prerequisite for an

upper-level course, "If you've passed Psychology 101, then you may take Psychology 201," this would activate your Permission schema. "If you water the plant, then it will grow" activates a Causal schema. People may then reason based on the schema activated (and even make reasoning fallacies that differ from schema to schema). These schemata are abstracted from everyday occasions and can then be applied to new situations. For example, your knowledge of the permission schema allows you to understand prerequisites even as a freshman who was never exposed to prerequisites *per se*.

ZAPS: WASON SELECTION TASK

Questions

1. Think of 5 conditional statements in the "If p, then q" format that you might encounter in real life.

2. Why do you think you found some of the problems in thise ZAP demo easier to solve than others? Did you have any sense of being able to detect the abstract or logical form of each problem after practicing on a few?

3. Should training in logic improve people's everyday reasoning skills? Would it improve their ability to critically assess advertisements and commercials? Why or why not?

ZAPS | Word Frequency

HOW TO: In this ZAP, you will be presented with a series of letter strings; some of them are words and some are nonwords. Press the **space bar**; a fixation string of asterisks will appear, followed by a string of letters. You must decide as quickly as possible whether each letter string is a word (and press the **m**-key) or a nonword (and press the **c**-key).

By the time we are teenagers, word recognition has become so rapid and so automatic that we barely pay attention to it. We don't even notice how quickly we recognize words until we run across an unfamiliar word when reading. Then, we may re-read the word and deliberately try to determine whether it is familiar, and whether we know the meaning.

Two issues arise—what does your word recognition system do if you run across a word that is unfamiliar, and that you don't even recognize as a word? Cognitively, you may scan your lexicon (or mental dictionary) and get to the end (figuratively) without matching the unfamiliar word to anything you have stored in memory. However, since you must scan memory longer before deciding conclusively that it is a word you don't know, the process will take longer than when you are confronted with a familiar word.

Secondly, are we as efficient at recognizing words that we don't use very often as words that we do use often? This is the issue of word frequency. Low-frequency words include words like *synergy* or *kaleidoscope* that we don't encounter often. High-frequency words include *money* and *weather* that we read or hear regularly. When we read, our eyes linger longer over low-frequency words. When performing a lexical decision task—deciding whether a string of letters is a word or not—less frequent words have longer response times.

One explanation for why low-frequency words take longer to recognize is that each word we know has a recognition *threshold,* for the amount of cognitive "energy" it takes to activate that word (and thus recognize it). The more often we see a word, the less energy it takes to activate it the next time, and the next time, and the next time. Thus, in lexical decision tasks, we can make faster judgments about high-frequency words. Low-frequency words, which we have encountered less frequently, have higher thresholds and thus require more energy to activate (resulting in longer response times).

In addition, immediately after reading a word, activation of that word within the lexicon takes a little while to fade. Thus, if you are presented with the same word a short time later, some activation still remains, and you will be even faster to recognize that word the second time. This is known as **repetition priming** and is a common effect in lexical decision tasks.

ZAPS: WORD FREQUENCY

Questions

1. What other factors do you think might influence how quickly we can activate or recognize words?

2. How long do you think repetition priming might last? One hundred milliseconds? One second? One minute?

3. When might we mistake a nonword for a word? When it sounds like a real word? When it looks like a real word except for one missing letter?

| Word Superiority Effect

HOW TO: Focus on the middle of the screen. In each trial, a word or letter will appear quickly. It will be replaced by a grid covering where the word/letter appeared. Underneath will be 3 dashes and an asterisk, plus a choice as to which of 2 letters (e.g., *u* or *a*?) had appeared in the place of the asterisk. Either click on the correct response or type the correct letter as quickly as you can.

For example, if *spot* appears, then "- - - *, *t* or *g*?," you would type *t* because that is the letter that had appeared in the fourth position of the stimulus (*spot*). There are 5 practice trials, then 36 regular trials.

A friend shows you a black-and-white picture that first appears to be just a mottled array of dots. Then your friend says, "See—it's a picture of a Dalmatian. Here's its head. . . ." Suddenly, the picture makes sense. That array of dots in the corner is the dog's head; the column of dots is its leg. Why were you able to discern the different parts of the dog only after your friend told you what the picture depicted?

Perception is based not only on the quality of a stimulus itself, but also on what we already know or expect from the stimulus. That is, both **bottom-up processing** (using what we actually see when we look at the Dalmatian picture) *and* **top-down processing** (what we expect to see, based on our knowledge of what a dog looks like) both affect our interpretation of a stimulus.

The **word superiority effect** is based on a classic experiment by Reicher (1969). As in the ZAP experiment, he presented people with an individual letter (*d*), or a string of random letters (*orwd*), or a legitimate word (*word*) very rapidly. A **mask** then appeared to cover the spaces where the letters had been as well as a 2-letter choice underneath one of the letter slots. Subjects had to decide which of the 2 letters had appeared in that letter slot (e.g., "*d* or *k*?" would appear in the fourth slot).

If bottom-up processing dominates letter recognition, then subjects should have been fastest and most accurate at recognizing an individual letter (*d*). After all, in the letter condition, there is only one fourth of the information to process as there is in the other 2 conditions. However, Reicher found that people were faster and more accurate at recognizing a letter that *had appeared in a word* than at recognizing the letter by itself. This finding supports top-down processing.

Top-down processing in letter recognition is assumed to occur in the following way: We know that our visual system first processes individual features of letters (the / - \ features of the capital letter *A*, for example). Activation of these individual features then activates letters composed of those features (*A*). In the word condition, activation of all four letters causes activation of the word itself. Top-down processing occurs at this level— activation of the word reinforces that the person saw the component letters of that word. Hence, the letter is more highly activated in the word condition than in the single-letter condition because of feedback from the word level.

Some researchers have argued that recent work on the phenomenon of change blindness is another example of top-down processing. People are shown a scene in a video. As the frames unwind, they do not detect significant changes to the scene, even when they are warned that there will be changes! For instance, one of the actors in the scene might change clothes, or the balcony behind a couple eating lunch might change position. In a real-life enactment of change blindness, Simons and Levin (1997) had an experimental confederate ask directions of students on the Cornell University campus. While the student was giving directions, some workmen carried a door between the student and the direction-asker (allowing the person asking directions to be replaced with a different person of a different height, build, clothing, and haircut). Only 50% of the students even noticed that they were now talking to a different person. Apparently, what we expect to see can override what is in front of our eyes.

ZAPS: WORD SUPERIORITY EFFECT

Questions

1. Top-down processing has been well confirmed using verbal stimuli. Do you think it would influence recognition of the component parts (nose, eye) of an object (a face), or the component objects (bicycle) in a scene (a schoolyard)?

2. Before the days of spell-checkers in word-processing programs, students were warned to read their papers backwards to check for spelling errors in their term papers. How can you explain why this advice was given, using what you now know about top-down processing?